Ballroom Fever

A strictly love affair

The George Lloyd Story

by George Lloyd

Clink
Street

London | New York

Published by Clink Street Publishing 2020

ISBNs
978-1-913568-06-1 (paperback)
978-1-913568-07-8 (ebook)

For my love – my wife Alyson who has helped me remember many things I had long forgotten.

Foreword

by Len Goodman

I owe so much to George Lloyd, much more than you would imagine, but more about that later.

Saturdays have always played a big part in my life. On a Saturday night back in 2004, *Strictly Come Dancing* began. Who would have thought it would become such a massive hit throughout the world, and I would become Head Judge? I still pinch myself now after all these years. One of my earliest memories is Saturday morning pictures, paying my sixpence and being one of the first ones in so I could sit in the front row. As a child, Saturday night was 'fish and chip' night. Going with my dad to the local chippy and rushing back in case they got cold. As a teenager, going to the Embassy Ballroom in Welling, Kent, on a Saturday night and jiving the night away – well to nine o'clock as I had to be home by 9.30 pm – was the highlight of the week.

Now back to how George Lloyd changed my life – in 1978 *Saturday Night Fever* was the big film of the year, and I went to see it and thought the music and the dancing was just fantastic. I thought maybe I should teach all the dances from the film at my studio in Kent, and so I went to learn the moves from George at the Sydney Francis Studio in Hendon, North London. I knew George from meeting him for many years at judging events and before that at

Phyllis Haylor Dance School in Hammersmith, London, where, like George, I trained for my ballroom teaching theory. I followed George's instructions to the letter, even down to the advert 'Seen the film, heard the music, now learn the dances'. Thanks to George, my dance studio was packed out. From one planned class a week, we ended up teaching *Saturday Night Fever* five nights a week! The dance classes went on long after the film had finished. In fact, we still teach Disco but it's now called 'Freestyle' to this day. Without knowing and visiting George I may not have become the teacher I was and then may not have had the opportunity of *Strictly Come Dancing* and all the other great opportunities that the programme has brought me since being involved as Head Judge. I'm truly blessed.

I lost touch with George and Alyson once they moved to Holland but what a joy this book had been to read, as it's taken me back to a life full of ups and downs, just like all of us.

George Lloyd has been, and still is, one of my dancing heroes.

I owe a lot to George Lloyd and hopefully this book will give you an in sight into his wonderful and colourful life.

Thanks to my Biographers

BOYD CLACK and KIRSTEN JONES – my Biographers have been amazing with regards to writing this book using their talent as professional writers to turn all my hand written notes into a readable form. Boyd's own autobiography 'Kisses Sweeter Than Wine' was published by Parthian followed by his later memoir 'Head in the Clouds: Memories and Reflections' in 2018. Also an actor, screen writer, raconteur, patron of a number of Welsh charities, this man has endless talents.

KIRSTEN JONES had the very complex task of co writing and editing the book and interrogating me on every detail which she did with a very positive and professional attitude. Kirsten is also an actor but perhaps they are both best known as the creators and script writers of the 6 Series of the highly successful BBC Wales sit com 'High Hopes' now on BBC iplayer. Kirsten is also patron of various charities including Royal Commonwealth Society of Wales, Cardiff Mini Film Festival, Greyhound Rescue Wales. They live in Cardiff with their cats.

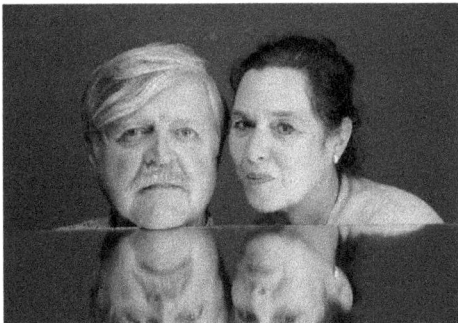

BOYD CLACK & KIRSTEN JONES
Photo courtesy of Twm Gardiner

Contents

Chapter 1   *'Son of my father'*   1

Chapter 2   *'Born to Hand Jive'*   11

Chapter 3   *'Red Roses for a Blue Lady'*   22

Chapter 4   *'Play Misty for me'*   33

Chapter 5   *'Tears of a Clown'*   46

Chapter 6   *'That's Life'*   57

Chapter 7   *'Spirit in the Sky'*   87

Chapter 8   *'The first time ever I saw your face'*   97

Chapter 9   *'Staying Alive'*   110

Chapter 10   *'How Deep Is Your Love'*   120

Chapter 11   *'Disco Inferno'*   132

Chapter 12   *'Candle in the Wind'*   145

Author's Supplement Guide to Judging   161

Chapter 1

'Son of my father'

I was born in Essex in 1955. My father Alfred Lloyd was fifty four years old and my mother Mollie was nineteen. My Dad was from the East End of London, a rough, working class part of the city where angels feared to tread. When my granddad Arthur, my mum's father, found out that his relatively unsullied little girl had been impregnated by a much older man he was understandably furious. Not so much at my mum who was little more than a child but at my dad who was 'a dirty bastard'. My granddad found out that she had met him in a nearby park and had word sent that he would like to meet him in the same park that evening 'to discuss the matter.' The 'discussion' would involve a beating the likes of the daughter defiling bastard had never had before. Disputes were often settled by violence in the East End in those days. Arthur turned up a few hours later as the sun was setting to find Alfred waiting for him. Though my dad was a tough looking man who no-one in their right mind would choose to pick a fight with, Arthur's righteous anger made him a fearsome prospect. In fact Arthur wasn't frightened of Dad at all having been a decorated war veteran. Neither man was a pussy. It could have been very nasty, very nasty indeed but what happened was that the two men did actually 'discuss the matter' and Arthur saw that Alfred was not the bastard he assumed him to be but that he genuinely loved his daughter and was committed to her and the as yet unborn child. The confrontation ended up with the two men shaking hands and going to a nearby pub for a pint together. My mum told me this story. My mum was lovely. She was so kind. She was the light of my life.

My grandfather on my dad's side was named George like me and he'd been a barber less than a mile from 'The Blind Beggar' pub in London's East End. My Nan, Rosie, had been a Music Hall singer in her younger days under the name of Rosie Lloyd. There were posters in the house advertising her appearances on Variety Bills. One had an old fashioned photograph of her on it, one of those where the colours looked faded. She was in a long white dress with a frilly front, wearing a delicate little hat and holding a parasol. She was billed as 'Rosie Lloyd the Camden Nightingale'. She used to sing around the house and her voice was very beautiful. My favourite song of hers was one called 'The boy I love is up in the gallery'. I used to think it was about me.

Dad's sister, my Auntie Gladys, owned a well known pub called The Dick Whittington. It was a roughhouse frequented by local layabouts and petty criminals. A strange and macabre incident paralleling the meeting between my granddad and dad in the park took place there in 1965, a short time before my family moved home. Auntie Gladys said that dad, who was a licensed bookmaker by profession, had got into some kind of trouble with a local criminal. This was when the Krays ruled the roost in the East End and this man was a well known thug, an animal as Gladys put it. Anyway he visited the pub and let it be known that he would be waiting down by the docks after stop tap and expected my dad to be there too or else. Dad was in no doubt that this would end up badly. As he left The Whittington,

Gladys saw him pick up an half empty soda siphon from the bar and put it under his crombie coat. Dad turned up at the bar as usual the following day but neither the gangster nor the soda-siphon was ever seen again. The water was deep in that part of the river and the tides strong. The conclusion was drawn, generally accepted but never voiced. Like I say my dad was a tough man. That said he never hit me or my mum, never. If there was a barney brewing he'd put on his hat and coat and go for a walk.

My dad moved in to live with my mum and her parents at 40 Castle Lane, Essex before I was born and the couple were given the ground floor front room as their own. It was a large room with recesses either side of the fireplace to the left a huge double wardrobe and to the right a kitchen dresser, table and three chairs. There was a dressing table in the bay window and my parent's double bed nearby with my single bed attached. It was crowded but it never seemed oppressive. There was an old black telephone and every time it rang my dad would say 'Don't answer it. It might be the police!' It never failed to make me laugh.

As I said my dad was a licensed bookmaker under the name of George Pickering and when I was young in the 60's he'd often take me around the racecourses with him and my uncles Harry and Ted. They'd put a 'pony' float in a leather bag before leaving the house and the bag would fill up with more cash during the day. At the start of each race I'd be sent to the bar to collect their beers. After the last race the bag would be slammed shut and we would make a quick exit to the car. On the drive home we'd always stop at The Wheatsheaf Pub where a lot more beer would be quaffed as the money was totted up and the share out took place. I'd sit there with my glass of lemonade and bag of Smiths crisps with a little blue bag of salt watching and my dad would say to me 'Son, this is why you should never gamble. Only the bookies win. It's a mug's game.' If only he'd listened to his own advice, God bless him. Dad had his scrap metal business too but though he earned a decent amount he was it seemed, like many men of the time, addicted to gambling and drink so we were always poor. On Sundays me and my dad would be driven to a country club by my uncle Eric in his Daimler Jaguar Mk11. Eric, a somewhat shady business-man, was known to one and all as 'One Way Eric' and was well off by our standards. He and my dad would get ham-mered on beer with whiskey chasers on these outings and Eric would regale the rest of the clientele with his opinions on various matters of philosophical and topical interest like a circus master in the centre of the ring. He was a friendly, jovial man and no-one objected, in fact they seemed to look forward to it. He had a number of 'businesses', car sales, a wood yard, scrap yard and several shops selling various goods. He had his fingers in many pies. One day when I was twelve, I discovered a black leather toilet bag at the bottom of my wardrobe. I unzipped it to find something wrapped in newspaper. It was a hand gun. I asked my Dad about it and he said he was looking after it for a friend. A few weeks later driving back from the country club Eric stopped off to buy some flowers for his wife and my mum. My Dad bought some strawberries. When Eric opened the car boot to put the flowers in I saw the black leather toilet bag lying next to a crowbar. I said nothing. I just thought of the song 'Silence is Golden'.

The rest of our house was occupied by the extended family. My Nan lived downstairs out the back. Jim, Trevor, Burt and Bill my four uncles lived upstairs in a room next to Auntie Rina, my mum's sister and, as I said, we were down-stairs front. It was a strange thing when you think of it that my dad was seventeen years older than my Granddad but it didn't seem to bother anyone. The boys sometimes called dad 'old timer' to pull his leg but he just laughed. I discovered that though he was of a generation that could have seen action in both World Wars my dad didn't fight in either. He was just not called up in WW1 and his job collecting scrap metal was considered vital for the war effort WW2. He wouldn't have minded joining up but it didn't work out that way. My Granddad was in The Essex Infantry in WW2 and was sent to France four days after D Day. He saw action in France, Belgium and Germany but never suffered a scratch. He told me that his best friend Fred Richardson committed suicide when they were in Germany. They'd relieved a concentration camp, not one of the famous ones, just a run of the mill place and Fred had killed some guards, shot them and the incident played on his mind till he took his gun one evening walked into a wood and blew his brains out. Granddad said that there were a surprising number of front line soldiers who killed themselves but it wasn't talked about because of the effect it would have on morale both in the army and at home. They were reported as killed in action. He didn't talk about the war much. I saw him crying once though, when we went to the flicks to see 'Tobruk', not sobbing his heart out just a few tears running down his cheeks.

As a girl my Mum had had to look after her three younger brothers as well as cooking and cleaning. My uncles told me that she had been wonderful but was virtually a slave. It made me sad to think of it. My Nan was loving and kind to me and I have only fond memories of her, however she did enjoy a very active social life and was rarely home. She loved Bingo and one armed bandits. Jim Haddow her new husband was a quiet man who read a lot. They seemed very happy together. As a matter of fact the whole house was a happy place. We lived in harmony and though we were poor I never felt poor. Lots of cuddles at bedtime, much love and laughter were riches enough for me. I was a happy little chap.

Where we lived was quite rural. At the bottom of Castle Lane is Hadleigh Castle which was built by Edward the Third in the thirteenth century. Next to it on the Salvation Army grounds was a farm. I spent a lot of time playing in the old castle. It was a magical place and few other kids ever went there. I liked being on my own. I was out in all weathers. I remember my mum lining the insides soles of my shoes with cardboard. It was fine till it rained and they got sodden. Our clothes were bought in jumble sales and our diet was poor working class, bread and dripping on Monday, tripe and cow heel once a week, cockles and winkles from Leigh on Sea as a Sunday treat and a big spoonful of Cod Liver Oil and Malt every morning. Dad brought home a turkey one day, a handsome chap who I soon befriended. His name was Wilfred, well that was the name I gave him and I loved him. I looked after him diligently feeding him every morning before school and then again when I got home. Christmas Day came and after dinner I went into the garden as usual to feed him and he was gone. My Dad said we'd ate him. It didn't sit easy with me. I loved animals, I still do. It didn't sit easy. You should never eat something you are on first name terms with. As I said I never felt poor and it was only when I went to school and other kids taunted me I realised that that is what we were ... 'Your dad's an old man.', 'You live with your Gran.', 'Your clothes don't fit proper.' ... They say that children can be cruel well I'm living testament to that. The truth is they didn't like me and, with one or two exceptions, I didn't like them.

My dad also ran a demolition firm and he got a contract to demolish ninety-six houses, six shops and a cinema in Southend. The houses and the cinema went first. Dad decided to leave the betting shop and café until last, you can guess why! There were lots of items left abandoned in the cinema, hundreds of balloons, Christmas decorations and a life size ventriloquist's dummy, a cross between Ray Alan's Lord Charles and Chucky. That Christmas Eve dad thought it would be a laugh to bring 'him' home and sit him up on the outside toilet next to the Izal paper flapping in the breeze with the flickering lamp on the blink like a scene from a Hammer Horror film. My Nan was the unlucky victim of the prank and she nearly died of fright. I can see her now running into the house screaming in terror 'Help! Help, there's a dead man sitting on the toilet!!' Cruel maybe but very funny. Apart from eating Wilfred it was the best Christmas ever.

I started going to the pig farm down the lane. I soon got to know Harry who owned the place and he'd let me help with the mucking out and any other jobs that needed doing. I loved it. Pigs are beautiful animals with their lovely faces and gentle nature. People think they are dirty but nothing could be further from the truth. It's just that they live differently to us. They like being in mud and getting dirty. They don't think of dirt in the way we do that's all. If I wasn't a person I'd like to be a pig. Harry was a friendly chap and always gave good advice if I asked him about anything. Dad knew him from the pub and said he was a good bloke. He was happy enough to leave me in his care. At that time, when I was seven or eight, one of my regular jobs was taking the shopping lists to the greengrocer, butcher and baker which were near the church in Hadleigh where I went to Sunday school. There was no candlestick maker as far as I remember. One day I got a list from my Nan to take to Mr and Mrs Buttery the chemists. For some reason Auntie Rina thought it would be a laugh to dress me up as a girl using some of her and my mum's clothing. She put a ribbon in my hair and makeup on my face, lipstick, powder, red stuff on my cheeks and stuff on my eyes and eyelashes. It took ages for her to do it and when she'd finished the effect was quite dramatic. I even wore my Nan's shoes. The Buttery's laughed when they saw me and made a couple of humorous comments but I got the feeling that they were a bit perplexed at such strange behaviour. I didn't feel girlie at all. I felt OK about it though I've not indulged since.

I bumped into a girl I knew one afternoon as I was coming home from the shops with a tin of paint. Her name was Sally Ruffel and she was regarded as the prettiest girl in class. She asked me what the paint was for, it was for mum to paint the kitchen, and then invited me back to her house to play. I had to get home though. She asked me if I would go to the Dance Studio with her that evening. It was not the first time she'd asked, she'd been asking me for weeks, but I'd always passed on it. I said maybe and walked on. Though only eight or nine years old my male hormones must have started kicking in already and the thought of spending some time in Sally's company was not an unpleasant one. I'd even imagined kissing her but dance lessons! This was not an age of gender fluidity. Boys were boys and girls were girls. Boys played rough games and ran around and had fights, they did not go to dance classes. I was on the horns of a dilemma. I called into the piggery later that afternoon to see the new litter of twelve piglets that Victoria had had the previous weekend. They were absolutely gorgeous all pushing and crawling over each other to get a teat. Victoria was a very proud mum indeed. I took the opportunity to ask Harry if he thought that dancing was just for girls and he said definitely not. He said any bloke who thought that was doing himself a foolish disfavour because there was no better place to pick up girls than in dance halls and girls were always impressed if a boy could dance well. He said he'd met his wife in The Kursaal, a dancehall in

Southend on Sea, before the war. This was very interesting but what if the boys at school called me a queer. Bugger them he said, let them call you what they like. It'll be you who gets the girls who wouldn't look at them twice. Teddy boys were great dancers. They took pride in it and nobody thought they were queer. Nobody said it anyway. I believed Harry and decided to go to the Dance Studio to meet Sally that evening as she asked.

I went home and told my mum I'd decided to go to the class. She was surprised as I'd dismissed the idea on several previous occasions but I told her what Harry had said made me decide to give it a go. She insisted I had a bath to get rid of the smell of pigs, which I rather liked, but I obeyed accepting that it was not something that would impress a girl. Surprisingly dad backed Harry up. He too had been a dance hall lothario in his younger days and said it was good fun. He said I'd have to pay for the lessons myself though as times were tight. Mum whispered to me not to worry. She'd get the money somehow. I put on some non pig smelling clothes and hit the highway, well the lane, in my best Sunday shoes.

The Dance Studio was located upstairs above the Kingsway Cinema in Hadleigh. I got there as the other kids were getting into groups. The place was run by the instructors Marian Barber and her husband Bob. The first thing I noticed was that of the dozen or so students I was the only boy. Marian came over and I told her I would like to learn to dance. Sally had spotted me by then and was beaming her pretty smile across the room. I smiled back. My first ever dance was with Marian herself who wanted to see if I had any natural feel. We tried a waltz and despite her being a grown woman some inches taller than me it seemed all right. She seemed to think so anyway. We did a Cha Cha Cha next though I don't remember doing anything different to when I was doing the waltz. I noticed that the girls had taken a rest from their exercises and were stood watching me. I got nervous and stood on Marian's foot. She winced but assured me that it was fine. It wasn't the first time her foot had been stood on. The girls went back to practising under Bob's sergeant major like commands until a break was called. There was a wooden hatch with a table in front on which there were jugs of orange squash and plastic cups. The girls swarmed around as I got myself a drink. Sally had obviously told them about me and I was the object of great curiosity. I liked it. Bob then took me to one side and asked me a few questions, where I was from, if I'd done any dancing before, why I wanted to dance now. I answered truthfully except for why I wanted to dance. To be honest I didn't want to dance. I'd gone there on a whim but I couldn't say that to Bob. I said my mother thought it would keep me fit. Bob was a big man with an incredibly straight back and a loud booming voice. I was pleased and somewhat relieved to see that he didn't seem the slightest bit queer. Marian told me not to be intimidated by him. She said that his bark was worse than his bite. The girls were whispering and giggling as we returned to the dance floor but I pretended to ignore them.

When I got home I was well and truly knackered. This dance malarkey was hard work. I sat by the fire with mum drinking a mug of hot chocolate and moaning. It made her laugh. She wanted to know all about it but I was too tired to go into much detail. I said that it was OK but that was it. I wouldn't be going again. I'd given it a whirl but dancing wasn't for me.

Chapter 2

'Born to Hand Jive'

Having decided not to go dancing again I returned to my hobby at the pig farm. I told Harry that I had given it a try but didn't like it. He laughed and told me I should persevere. He took to spinning around the shed and doing the Jive with a mucking out rake as his partner. He'd throw himself into it like he was Little Richard. Sometimes he'd even dance with the pigs. It was very funny, made even funnier by the fact he was wearing wellington boots. I loved it. My mum, the girls from the class and the other women in the family egged me on too. The truth is though that all the persuading and nagging in the world wouldn't have worked if I hadn't for some reason become a little fascinated with dance. I wouldn't have called it fascination at the time but that one lesson had left me with a curiosity about movement. I found myself becoming aware of my body as I walked along, how it worked, flowed from place to place. I decided to give The Dance Studio another go. This time I really enjoyed it and before long I was a regular, dancing more and more with the girls and spending less and less time with the pigs.

Listen I have to explain something here, finding dance saved my life. Although I had a loving family and in truth wanted for little, there was, and always had been, an irrational, sometimes uncontrollable fear inside me. There are all sorts of psychological and psychiatric theories as to where such things come from but try as I might I have never figured it out in my case. Every time I went out I would have a feeling of uncertainty, regardless of whether I was attending school, going to the farm, shopping, or playing with friends. The anxiety could be mild or intense depending on what I was doing and where I was but it would always settle once I returned home, where I felt safe. Dance became a second refuge from the anxiety. I felt as safe at The Studio as I did at home. Like I said, it saved my life. I don't know if anyone is born for any specific reason or whether life just takes us where it will but if the former is true then, melodramatic as it may sound, I was born to dance. I have never felt happier or more alive than on the dance floor and for that I am blessed.

I came home from school one day when I was eight to find a cot with a baby brother in it. I had no idea how this had happened. It was like a miracle. My Nan said 'Your mum has had a baby. He's your brother. His name is Paul.' There were four of us living in the front room now but Paul was no bother. I liked him and quickly grew to love him. When he was a little bit older I'd take him for a walk in his pushchair every day. It was nice having a little person who looked a bit like me about. We were chums.

When Paul was two the council gave us a house on a rough estate in Benfleet about three miles from Nan's house. I had my own bedroom for the first time! It was small but perfect. I had a poster of Gene Kelly, who I had grown to worship after seeing him in 'An American in Paris' at the Kingsway with Sally, on my wall. I even considered changing my name to Gene for a time but shelved the idea when my mum said I should be proud of my own name, George. My mum was right.

I got a part time job in the local garage cleaning car wind-screens and checking oil and water. It was cold in the winter but I loved the chance to have a close up look at the different cars. I got a Saturday job in the local Market shop too. I used to take my mum presents like a new plastic washing up bowl or an ironing board or glass tumblers with different flowers painted on them. She loved these simple gifts and I loved the happiness they brought her. I gave her any money I had left over to help with the running of the house. My mum would still visit the jumble for clothes and the market for the cheapest food. She'd get home in the late afternoon and my dad would be asleep in his chair exhausted by his usual routine, a hard day's work, a visit to the betting shop and a hard drinking session in the pub. They both smoked heavily. I can remember hundreds of Embassy cigarette coupons stacked up on the sideboard. My mum was saving them for a new Hoover.

So at the age of ten I had two jobs and was now commit-ted to Ballroom Dancing. I'd even begun dancing in my dreams. I was addicted. Dance was the drug I was thinking of. I was dance crazy. When I was eleven I announced that I wanted to be a dance teacher. People laughed at first but I was deadly serious. I'd watched Marian and Bob teaching and I saw the immense joy it gave them. It seemed the most perfect job in the world to me. My dad once told me that to earn a good living from something you'd be doing even if you weren't getting paid for it was the secret of a happy life. He was talking about professional football at the time but the same applied to dance. I was determined even at that young age. Nothing was going to stop me ... nothing! At twelve I was helping teach the kids to dance on Saturday mornings. It only seemed like a few weeks ago that I was falling over my own feet, and now this.

From that time on I spent every minute I could at The

Studio. I moved up to the Secondary school and it was even worse than Junior. I hated it and would make any excuse not to go. I was not academic. Mathematics, history, geography and all of those things meant nothing to me, less than nothing. I skived off regularly. When I did go I was invariably late because I would have worn myself out at dance class the night before. I'd fall asleep at my desk. The teachers, who didn't like me much in the first place, began to hate me. They couldn't see that I wasn't like the others. I was a dancer, an artist. The mediocrity of their world was not for me. On top of this existential impasse I'd become the subject of constant bullying. The other boys were idiots in the main but one or two were really nasty bits of work and they took against me because I was quiet which in their eyes meant that I considered myself superior to them, which of course I was. When it became known that I went to dance lessons it singled me out as a 'poof' too and poofs were fair game for everyone. My dad told me to go up to the biggest one, the biggest bully, the ringleader and punch him as hard as I could on the nose as many times as I could before I was dragged off. He said that all bullies were cowards and if you showed you could fight back they'd leave you alone. It's what he would do in my situation but I was not my dad. I went to school less and less. I kept away from them. My mum sympathised and would write me sick notes. She was very supportive of my decision to become a dance teacher. I went home one day and found a brand new pair of dancing shoes in a swanky box on my bed. They were very expensive and I don't know how mum managed to afford them but she did. I'll never forget the feeling the first time I put them on. They were so soft, so light and the patent leather glistened like stars. I wore them day and night, including in bed, for a fortnight to break them in.

Around that time I went to see World Latin American

champions Laird and Lorraine performing at a small venue in Southend and a few weeks later I saw The Delroys at the same venue. These shows were amazing, to be there watching these incredible dancers, to see them up close like that, so perfect and refined beneath the dazzling lights. It was magical and it made me more determined than ever to have a career in dance. I had no idea then of course that I would work with Walter Laird one day or that I would have lessons from John Delroy but I did know that this was a world I craved to be a part of.

I continued to study hard and trained for my first Student teachers exam. I took the exam with the Imperial Society of Teachers of Dancing London, at the age of fourteen and was successful. It was 1969, the year after the student riots in Paris, the year The Beatles broke up and the Americans landed on the moon. I'd begun to relate to the outside world. I'd been too young to experience the Swinging 60's first-hand but some of it had inevitably seeped in. I'd heard about hippies and marijuana and free love but I had no first-hand experience of any of them. I was particularly interested in the free love bit. When I'd go to bed at night I'd dream that I was having steamy sex with a bevy of beautiful nymphets. It was the first thing I'd come across that rivalled dancing for fun. I was getting plenty of one but none of the other.

By 1970 I had begun taking adult learners classes at The Studio. Sally assisted me for the experience. One evening I was meeting a beginner's class of about forty couples when I saw that my school's head teacher Mr Jones and his wife were among them. Needless to say they were surprised to see me in my role as a dance instructor but I greeted them as any other learners and that helped relax the situation. Then I realised that Creepy Lambert my form teacher was in attendance too and that freaked me out a bit. Still I was a 'professional' and did my best to at least appear to take it in my stride. I began the session getting all the men to line up behind me and all the ladies behind Sally. I then took them through the basic foot positions for the waltz … 'Gents, right foot forward on the heel. Ladies, left foot back keeping the toe in contact with the floor. Gents, left foot to the side, both commence rising onto the toes. Gents close right foot to left, Ladies close left foot to right and continue to rise on both toes.' Some of the pupils were getting it. A few were losing their balance and falling into each other. This was normal. They were all enjoying themselves however and that is a prerequisite to learning. We continued with the individual exercises for half an hour or so, then they partnered up. I counted the beat out loud to 'Moon River' by Andy Williams, a perfect waltz number for beginners. 'Now listen for the beat. I'll count you in, begin after three. 1,2,3 and 1,2,3 and 1,2,3, that's it, keep going! 1,2,3 …' There was an audible excitement from the dancers when it ended. They were proud of themselves. I told them that they had done well and now there'd be a twenty minute break for refreshments from the bar. It was then that Sally pointed out that Creepy was there with Jennifer Moses who was a pupil in our class. I thought it was just that maybe he wanted to learn and his wife didn't so Jennifer offered to partner him but then I saw them holding hands so it was pretty clear that something was afoot. Creepy was in his forties and Jennifer was so young. It didn't seem right but I put it out of my mind and carried on with the second half of the lesson which was the basic Cha Cha Cha. The evening had been a success and I got a lot of very positive comments from my pupils. I was getting better and better as a teacher every session. I was born for this.

The next day at school Creepy asked me to stay behind for a private word after registration. He told me that he was surprised to see me taking the dance class and he'd like to explain that he'd gone to The Studio with Jennifer for the very reason I had assumed. His wife knew all about it, she encouraged it in fact. Though she had no interest in learning herself she liked him to have a hobby. He asked me not to speak about it though because people might get the wrong idea. I told him I had no interest in gossiping about my dance pupils and he thanked me. He was satisfied with this declaration and told me that in that case he and Jennifer would continue with the lessons. He added that I was an extremely impressive teacher and that he would mention it to the Barbers. Our conversation being over I went on to my morning class. From that day on I never got another late mark or row for not attending school and as promised the teachers, and Jennifer, continued classes at The Studio. On my final school report he commented 'If this young man had put the same amount of effort into his school work as he did with his ballroom dancing he would be a genius. I sincerely wish him well for the future.' A few years later Creepy left his wife and children and set up home with Jennifer. It was a huge scandal at the time. Looking back he was my teacher and Mr and Mrs Jones accompanied them to lessons so I had to assume everything was alright. It seemed odd but nothing huge, nothing dramatic. Creepy and Jennifer remained together for the rest of his life so there must have been something genuine there.

A few months later I experienced something similar myself. I had noticed that some of my female pupils had been taking more than a professional interest in me during and after lessons. It was very nice but I was young and nervous, terrified of humiliating rejection as all young people are and I found myself incapable of taking advantage of the situation. One Saturday after a class a girl student, a young woman really, she was twenty years old, named Ulrika Turner asked me if

I'd like to go to the Pictures with her that evening. I said yes. Ulrika was a dish, raven black hair, sleepy eyes and luscious lips. She was a young boy's erotic fantasy and she had been the object of my secret lust from the moment I first laid eyes on her. I met her outside the flicks and we got two seats near the back. I was wearing my new suit, a dark blue, velvety off the peg that I had seen in a shop window and fallen in love with. I felt cool. Ulrika was wearing a tight pink sweater and a black skirt. She looked stunning. The film was 'Get Carter', a British gangster movie with Michael Caine in the lead. About ten minutes into the film Ulrika put her hand on my thigh and started kissing me, real kissing, necking. I could taste her lipstick and smell her breath. It was fantastic. After a few minutes her hand moved up my leg. Finally she took me by the hand and rushed me up the stairs to the empty projection booth so quickly I thought the place must have been on fire and there, while Michael Caine was getting Britt Ekland to talk dirty on the screen and lit by the flickering film light we consummated our passion on the red carpeted floor. It was the most romantic moment of my life. Ulrika and I became an item and I finally got to do what I had dreamt of doing for a thousand lonely nights.

After the film we kissed goodbye on the cinema steps and I began to walk home. It was a cold late night with a clear sky full of stars. I was floating in the air. I had never felt happier. About half way back I was confronted by a large gang of boys. I recognised some from school, the others were estate boys and they were wild with drink. I put my head down and tried to ignore them but they'd seen me and crossed the road to have some fun at my expense. The leader was a right bastard named Mike Scaratt. He blocked my path. 'Well if it isn't Rudolf fuckin' Nuree-eff!' He said. 'Show us a bit of dancin' then you poof.' The others laughed at his witticism. I tried to push past. 'Don't push past me you fuckin' arse bandit.' he said, 'I told you to fuckin' dance. We all want to watch you dance and wiggle your arse about don't we boys! You like that don't you?' The others were circling me and egging Scaratt on. One of them shouted 'Thump the fucker Mike!' and that is what he did. He punched me hard in the stomach and I bent double. I knew that worse was to come so I punched him back aiming for his nose as dad had told me. I connected and his nose burst and spouted blood. Scaratt was stunned. He really hadn't expected it. Neither had I come to that. I have no idea where it came from. Once Scaratt had recovered from his initial shock he started dancing around me aiming more punches and I returned him blow for blow'. I was beyond frightened. I was angry and filled with hate. The gang were cheering Scaratt on until I caught him a really solid punch to the side of the head and he fell backwards onto the road. A strange bewildered silence descended. I stood waiting for him to get up but instead after kneeling and wiping the blood off on his jacket sleeve he turned to his acolytes and screamed 'Well, what the fuck are you waitin' for … Kill the bastard!' And the gang immediately fell on me like a pack of dogs, punching and kicking me from every angle. I fell to the floor and curled into a ball but the blows continued to rain for what seemed an eternity. I felt the dull thuds of boot and fist falling like distant rain all over my body. One of the dogs hit me over the head with a full beer bottle which broke and splintered and showered pale ale down my shirt and over my face. I lay there unmoving unable to defend myself any longer listening to the blows and the laughter and the swirling pagan sounds of their delight until finally the face of the mighty Scaratt appeared above me, framed by the black starlit sky. He looked into my eyes for a moment, said 'Night, night you poof.' and kicked me as hard as he could in the face. I didn't hear or see anything after that.

I don't know how long it took but I came to, eventually and managed to stagger to my feet. It was still dark. I headed home leaning against walls and shop windows for support and somehow managed to get there before collapsing in the hallway. My mum and dad had been worried. It was very late. I told them what had happened and they were horrified. Mum grabbed a poker to go and find the gang but I told her they were well gone. Dad inspected my battered face and looked at my chest which was covered in blue black bruises. He phoned for the doctor. I had a broken nose, two black eyes and three cracked ribs ... and oh yes, my new suit was ruined. It took me a good three weeks to recover which I spent in bed entertaining visitors. I don't know what happened but I was never picked on again after that even though I saw some of the boys, including Scaratt again on more than one occasion. I have a suspicion that dad paid the families a visit. Getting beaten up like that is a terrible thing. It's not like you see in films. It's savage and visceral, man at his most primitive. The physical scars heal but the mental ones never do. I am nervous of going out after dark to this day.

1971 was a year of rioting in Northern Ireland, bombs planted by The Angry Brigade in London and the release of the seventh James Bond film, 'Diamonds Are Forever'. I was sixteen, no longer a virgin and now a fully fledged teacher of Ballroom Dance.

I had been coaching young learners for the Medal Test Exam which was to be judged by two examiners from London. This involved the learners doing a dance I had choreographed and practiced with them with me as their partner for them to assess. There was a session in the morning and another in the afternoon. On the day the morning session went particularly well and after a quick cup of tea and sandwich I returned to The Studio ready to have an equally successful afternoon. Bob and Marian had taken the examiners out for lunch and when they got back Bob took me aside and told me that the talk at lunch had mainly been about me. Although not there to judge me the examiners had nonetheless been highly impressed by my teaching and dancing abilities. Young men of my talent and qualifications were few and far between in the world of professional dance in those days and one of the examiners, Major Teddy Edwards, an old school, ex military, stiff upper lip type, had told Bob that he would like to offer me a job teaching ballroom in London with Phyllis Haylor. I had no idea who Phyllis Haylor was and Bob explained that she was one of the leading ballroom teachers in the world having herself been World Ballroom Champion in 1926. I was flabbergasted. Bob explained that the Major had approached him and asked if he would agree to let me go from my job at the Studio to take up this new position out of professional courtesy and that although he and Marian didn't want to lose me that this was a great opportunity. He said he would never have forgiven himself if he hadn't passed the request on. Then he gave me a hug and said he and Marian were very proud of me. The afternoon session was if anything even better than the morning's. After I got changed I talked to the Major himself. He gave me his card and told me to ring and make an appointment to see Phyllis Haylor in London. Little did I imagine for one moment what lay ahead. This day was to propel my country boy, provincial life in a stunning new direction.

Chapter 3

'Red Roses for a Blue Lady'

The big day came and I was up early. I travelled from Benfleet to London by train and caught a bus to Mayfair. I had been to London before of course quite a few times to visit my dad's family but that had been to the East End which was shabby and run down. Mayfair was a different world, the noise of buses, cars and people rushing along, everything seemed to be going so fast. I made my way to 188, Hammersmith Road and arrived at Phyllis Haylor's famous Dance Studio in the Mardi Club. It was in a magnificent three story red brick Edwardian building with a shiny black door and four large white pillars outside. It looked like a Greek Temple. I eventually plucked up the courage to ring the doorbell and after a few moments The Major appeared. He seemed happy to see me, and invited me in. There was a long corridor with doors leading off. The Major told me to take a seat and that Miss Haylor would be out to see me shortly then he disappeared. The inside of the building was every bit as impressive as the façade. The corridor was lined with framed photographs of famous dance champions. I got up and walked up and down looking at them. They all looked so perfect, so elegant like people from a Fred Astaire film. I noticed that there was music playing from behind a closed set of double doors. It was 'Red Roses for a Blue Lady' by Vic Dana, a song I was familiar with. The song ended and I sat back down when I heard footsteps approaching from inside. The doors to the Ballroom opened and a middle aged couple appeared. They introduced themselves as Bill and his wife Bobbie. I told them my name and we shook hands. Then they sat down for a moment to change their shoes. That is when I realised that they were one of the couples in the photographs. Theirs was behind where they were sitting in a gold frame. They were Bill and Bobbie Irvine MBE, the former World Dance Champions. Bill asked me what I was studying. I told him about the interview. They wished me luck then left. A moment or so later the Ballroom doors opened again and Phyllis Haylor came through them. She was simply stunning, aged in her sixties, dressed in a diaphanous flowing gold gown, tall straight, immaculate in every detail. I had never seen anyone as exquisite in appearance in my life. She invited me to into the Ballroom for 'a little chat.' The Ballroom was huge with a lovely sprung maple floor and large mirrors on the walls. There were golden cherubs lining the cornices of the high ceiling and open skylights through which the sunlight was pouring in. At one end of the room there was a raised stage area incorporating a licensed bar cleverly concealed during the daytime by heavy gold velvet curtains. This was The Mardi Club itself. The Major was sat in front of the curtains at the far end in observation mode. He flicked a hand in recognition. Miss Haylor and I sat and talked. She wanted to know everything about me. I told her how much I loved dancing, I had never wanted to compete in competitions or become a champion; I wanted to teach and had an interest in choreography. I would rather help make a champion than become one. She said that showed a commitment to the art of dance, and that she liked my refreshing outlook then she went to the gramophone and put on 'Red Roses for A Blue Lady'. 'Let's try a Foxtrot dear.' We began to dance. My nerves soon settled, mainly due to the fact that whatever I did she just followed me, light as a feather in my arms, no resistance at all. It was like one body dancing with four legs. It felt truly amazing. At the corner where the doors were open I did a curved three step into backward feather steps. There with the added sounds of busy London, the music and the lovely smell of fresh cut flowers that adorned the tables around the bar I was in my heaven. I wanted to keep dancing forever but sadly the music ended. Miss Haylor smiled at me, 'That will do nicely dear. The job is yours.' I asked if she'd like to try another dance to make sure. She laughed. 'No I'm sure dear. You can start as soon as you find accommodation. Try the Burlington Bureau on the Broadway they have flats to let. Just go and flutter those big blue eyes!' I could have cried with joy.

I didn't waste any time. I went straight to The Burlington and fluttered the big blue ones as advised, it worked! They sent me on a bus ride to Niton Street off Fulham Palace Road to view a top floor bedsit at number six. I was shown around by the owner of the house, an old Jewish gentleman named Mr Mickalov. It was a surprisingly nice place, double bed, sideboard, wardrobe and the share of the bathroom with hot water for six pound a week. Anywhere nearer the dance studio would have been outside my price range. It felt safe. My anxiety level had been soaring out in this strange new world. I was worried about living on my own but the welcome I experienced from Mr Mickalov helped calm me. I told him I'd take it, gave him a week's rent in advance and it was mine. I found out later that Mr Mickalov was Polish and had escaped the Nazi takeover of the country and fled to England in 1941. He managed to buy the house and lived now on the income from letting out rooms. He was a kindly man with a gentle but worn face and sad eyes. You could tell that he had seen some terrible things in his time; that terrible things had happened to him. He was to become a good friend. I rushed back to the dance studio and told Miss Haylor I'd found digs already and gave her the address. She was impressed by my enthusiasm and told me I could start work the following Monday at thirty pounds a week! I was over the moon. I couldn't wait to get home and tell everyone.

Mum and Dad were delighted at the news, all the family were. Mum wanted to know everything about the interview. I told her about the studio. I said that it looked like a Hollywood film set and that Miss Haylor was the most amazing person I'd ever met, that she danced like Ginger Rogers and spoke like the queen. I described what she looked like, how she dressed, her perfume, her hair, her jewellery. Mum was enthralled. Dad warned me to watch out for myself in London. He said it could be a dangerous place if you mixed with the wrong sorts. I told him I'd be careful. I could hardly contain my excitement, London was so new, so thrilling. I had to go to the Studio to break the news to Bob and Marian. I phoned Ulrika and she was waiting in reception when I got there. She said that she was going to move to London to be with me. I was surprised, a little perplexed even, but on the plus side I wouldn't be alone, which would in turn help with my anxiety. The problem was that her parents wouldn't let her go unless we were married. I didn't know what to say. She waited in reception as I went into the Studio. There was a lesson in progress, about twenty couples doing a Rumba to 'Spanish Eyes' by Al Martino. I joined Bob, Marian and Sally on the stage. I told them the good news and they were happy for me but when I mentioned my conversation with Ulrika, Sally said I should do as she'd asked and marry her. I told her that I wasn't daft and had no intention of marrying anyone. I wasn't even sixteen! Bob called the interval and we had a drink to celebrate. Ulrika had joined us by then and when we were leaving she told me that she had decided to go to London with me no matter what her parents said and then she proposed. I was at a loss. I said I was still a boy and had no money but she didn't care. She said she loved me. I don't understand why to this day but I ended up saying yes. My dad drove me up to my digs on the Sunday and three weeks later I returned to Benfleet and, having turned sixteen just a few days earlier, married Ulrika at the local church. Her parents had arranged everything and all I had to do was say 'I do' and that was that. Like I said I had no idea how all this happened. I didn't love her and I didn't want to be married. I was swept along in events that seemed to have nothing to do with me. My new bride and I moved to London and I carried on with my work.

For the next six months I received intense training from Miss Haylor to prepare me for The Membership Exam. Although I was only sitting the Associate Exam at this stage Miss Haylor's philosophy was to be fully prepared and one step ahead of the game. I needed to be fully qualified to train a class of students from a special London college. Fortunately I received a special dispensation from the board of The Imperial Society of Teachers of Dancing to sit the Associate exam at the age of sixteen. I passed with distinction thus becoming the youngest person ever to qualify. I couldn't have done it without Miss Haylor. She had such faith in me. Though I had passed the exam I wouldn't officially receive the result and certificate until I was seventeen. I was informed of the results on the QT and had to promise not to tell anyone on pain of death. The following day Miss Haylor took me out for afternoon tea to celebrate. She drove us to Kensington in her royal blue Austin Princess Vanden Plas and parked outside The Royal Garden Hotel.

The inside was how I imagined Buckingham Palace to be. They greeted Miss Haylor effusively and the manager led us to her 'usual table'. She ordered 'two teas' but when the waiter brought them there weren't just two cups of tea there was a fantastic tall layered tray thing loaded with tiny sandwiches and tiny cakes too. When I commented on this Miss Haylor burst into laughter, she said that for her, afternoon tea would never be quite the same again. I didn't get it but I laughed along anyway to be polite. She told me that she was delighted and proud of my achievement and that I should be too but that I shouldn't let it go to my head. I assured her it wouldn't. The food was very nice but there wasn't that much of it. I said nothing. That day was the first day in my life anyone ever called me 'Sir'. Miss Haylor told me I'd have to get used to it.

Up until then I had been partnering somewhat elderly women hoping to improve their limited technique. They were refined and polite but there was no excitement to it, no challenge. Then things changed. The special London College turned out to be The Royal Academy of Dramatic Arts or RADA as it is generally referred to. Everyone knows about it now but then it was a very exclusive establishment. Since the film 'Fame', acting has become a popular, common even, choice of career for people from all walks of life but back then it was essentially confined to the affluent classes and RADA was their school of choice. One of the aspects of their teaching was dance and now, suitably qualified, I was designated to take the RADA ladies in their twice weekly classes to prepare them for their Ballroom Student Teachers Exams. The 'ladies' were aged eighteen to twenty one and the majority of them weren't interested in pursuing careers in acting or indeed any other dramatic art come to that. For them it was the equivalent of what was known as a finishing school, a place where they could hone their social skills and acquire some knowledge of life. They were all beautiful and refined. They all wanted to be admired and lusted after. They were English Roses waiting to be plucked! The lessons were steamy and fun but the problem was that my new wife had decided to attend them as an observer. I didn't want her there but she didn't care what I did or did not want and came anyway. She started to accuse me of flirting with the girls. I explained that dance is a very physical thing and that the impression of romance is an integral part of many styles but she couldn't or wouldn't see it. Shortly after she straight out accused me of 'sleeping with all the girls' from RADA behind her back. She was screaming at me and crying and swearing. It was crazy. I told her that I was either in the Studio or in the bedsit twenty-four hours a day, it was impossible for me to be 'sleeping with' anyone behind her back or even in front of it come to that but she wouldn't listen. She left me and returned to her parents in Essex the next day. The last time I ever saw her was when she got on to the train at Fenchurch Street. We'd been married for five months. The truth was that I had been railroaded into marriage by a girl I didn't really know. She wanted a home, a family and a comfortable middle class life and thought that I could provide these things. Why she thought this I have no idea. I certainly said or did nothing to give her that impression. I never lied to her, she knew that I was committed to dance but I think her confidence in her ability to control me was such that she just ignored my plans and desires and convinced herself I'd fall into line but quite frankly I wasn't ready to settle down and have children as she had wanted. The truth of the matter was that I was still a child myself. We remained technically married but separated for the then requisite three years and when they had elapsed her parents arranged our divorce. All I had to do was sign a form.

Though glad to be out of my marriage I nonetheless felt a bit low. Miss Haylor, who knew of my divorce, picked up on my mood and invited me for tea at her home in Mayfair. It was sheer elegance with luxurious furnishings the likes of which I had never seen before. She unpacked the Harrods shopping bag and shortly after served tea in a silver teapot with bone china cups and saucers and a silver tower of cakes and sandwiches fit for a king. She asked me how I was feeling. Well it wasn't my heart it was the anxiety of being alone a selfish thing really. Miss Haylor understood and gave me some good advice. When you feel lonely at night just think about the morning, your pupils will be waiting for you, the music, the dancing, the exciting day ahead. Cuddle your pillow and smile as you imagine all the wonderful things in your life. 'Tea 'n sarnies' never tasted so good.

It didn't take me long to acquire some good friends in the Mardi Club circle, Miss Haylor of course and her close friend Nerina Shute and ex World Latin Champion Leonard Patrick who as well as teaching also shared the running of The Mardi Club with The Major, were the closest. Lenny was upper class and very stylish and, having seen and experienced first-hand all the difficulties, insecurities and jealousies of the professional dancing world, now had a laid back wisdom that he was happy to share. He was very funny too and oh yes he was gay as indeed was Miss Haylor and her close friend, the charming Nerina. I have never had any problem with people being homosexual, male or female. Although not gay myself I even somehow identified with them. They were outsiders like me. Lenny, Miss Haylor and Nerina were in fact the first 'out' gay people I had ever actually met and they were kind, friendly and fascinating. It made me think about Benfleet and the boys who beat me up. They hated gays despite quite probably never having met one in their limited lives. It seemed ridiculous. Surely there were better things to spend their energy on. Maybe they were frightened of their own feelings in this regard. Maybe they were beating themselves up. Whatever the case, I was not like them. I take people for what they are. Lenny was a damned good bloke.

Kind and supportive though she was Miss Haylor was a hard taskmaster in every way. She had determined to smooth out my rough country boy manners and speech for instance and was forever picking me up on my dropped H's. Over a period of time her persistence began to pay off and I became more confident in company. My anxiety became less intrusive. Since Ulrika had left me, I had been bedding the RADA girls and others like a kid in a candy shop and that is indeed what I was. I was on a sparkling merry go round and it was absolutely wonderful. Listen, all young men think of virtually nothing else but sex. It's quite simply a fact. If you are a man you'll know this. I couldn't look at a girl without wanting to get her in the sack and my job had them passing in front of me on a conveyor belt, blond, brunette, tall, short, brainless or smart, all willing. Take your pick. It was the age too, the early seventies, the dolly bird mentality, the pill, the live for today ethos and the drugs, not that I ever indulged but they were always around in those circles, created a Wonderland of promiscuity. I became a familiar face on the scene. My self confidence was also reinforced by a magical elixir I had discovered. It was colourless and came in a clear glass bottle. It was called Smirnoff. Yes the booze came into my life like another lover. It trickled over my lips and kept me warm at night. Lenny took me around the 'in' places and introduced me to their inhabitants. Benfleet was a million miles away. This was a whole new glittering world for me to explore. I drank it all in with the vodka and lime. I didn't have any second thoughts about my behaviour. I didn't think at all. I just put my arms out wide and fell forward.

Lenny took me out on the town one night and we ended up in the infamous Purple Pussy Club, I kid you not, that is what it was called! It was packed as it always was and my memory of it was a never ending kaleidoscope of pretty girls, vodka and dance. Dancing as Harry and dad had assured me was indeed a magnet to party girls and it wasn't long before I met Holly on the dance floor and at the end of the night her and her friend came back to my place. Holly was a bright girl who worked in a shop in Oxford Street. She was still there lying next to me wearing nothing but my shirt when I woke in the morning. The other young lady was making coffee and toasting crumpets for us. This was the life!

Then out of the blue I received some devastating news. My mum rang and told me that she had left my father. She had found a new bloke, taken Paul and gone off to live with him. On top of this I discovered that she and dad had never in fact been officially married. Lenny told me that that didn't really matter and of course it didn't but I had grown up thinking that they were and …. I was at a loss. I knew that my dad would be in a hell of a state and I got the next train back to Essex.

When I got home I found dad sat in his armchair by the unlit fire in the living room. It was dark, the curtains were drawn. I could see he had been crying. I tried to comfort him but didn't really know what to say. He told me that things hadn't been right between them for some time. It was that she was so much younger, thirty five and as time went on and he entered into old age, he was seventy now, they drifted apart. He wasn't angry. He said he could see it from her point of view. She still had a life ahead of her. She wanted some happiness. She wanted love not that he didn't love her, but it was a love devoid of romance, an old man's love. She had just had enough. She had to save herself. Dad was very sad but I also detected a sort of relief. He wanted for her what she wanted for herself. It may have been an old man's love but it was beautiful and poignant. We sat and cried together. He had a contact number for my mother and I arranged to meet her in a café in town the next day. She was trying to be matter of fact but I could see she was very upset by what had happened too. Her story tallied with dad's more or less exactly. She'd been with dad since she was nineteen and never really experienced the things most young women experienced. At first she thought it didn't matter but as time passed she began to realise that it did. She thought dad being so much older didn't matter either but she was proven wrong again. She didn't blame dad. He'd always been good to her but there were some things he couldn't satisfy especially as he grew older. Though it remained unsaid we were both aware that she was talking about sex. It wasn't just that of course, it was a feeling that she was trapped, that her life was slipping away. She told me she'd been feeling it for years. I didn't know what to say. She'd met this new bloke and he made her feel alive again. She told me she loved him. I knew a bit about sex but nothing about love, not the love between a man and a woman I mean. Sex was an uncontrollable wild thing but love, that sort of love… well I supposed that it was overwhelming, irresistible. It had to be. I kissed mum goodbye and caught the train back to London.

Chapter 4

'Play Misty for me'

When I got back to The Mardi I threw myself into my work. It helped me cope with my sadness and confusion over mum and dad's break up. You can get lost when you are dancing. The outside world fades into the ether. At the end of the day's lessons around eight o' clock the social dance evening would begin. Lenny would open the bar behind the curtains; pour two vodka and limes with lots of ice for me and him and a G&T for Elsa Wells a fellow teacher who would usually join us. She was a famous figure in the world of ballroom and I got to know her well. I always looked forward to that part of the day. Lenny and Elsa made me laugh and forget my worries. I'd tell them jokes too which they enjoyed, the ruder the better. Elsa would take her handkerchief to pat her eyes whilst Lenny would laugh and shake his head and say "Oh Georgie, Georgie, Georgie!" I think they found my working class sense of humour a sort of guilty delight. Sometimes I'd do impersonations of other dancers, their walks, their mannerisms and voices. I'd have them saying outrageous, often disgusting, things. Elsa loved it. Sometimes Miss Haylor would arrive early and catch me at it. She'd say "Having another little party Ducky." which meant 'Open the curtains and start behaving yourself.' I would obey and spend the rest of the evening dancing with the clientele like Prince Charming but then at the end of the night Lenny would allow a selected few friends to stay behind for drinks and I'd revert to my Norman Wisdom mode again, more booze, laughter and another late night. My gloom began to dissipate.

The following Saturday Miss Haylor arranged a special party evening with a demonstration by her close friends Ballroom World Champions Peter Eggleton and Brenda Winslade. I had previously seen them dance at the Hammersmith Palais but watching them dance in the Mardi, a much smaller venue, was extra special. They danced syncopated natural pivots with his tails flying and her dress swishing as they passed in front of me. With the soft sound of their feet skimming across the surface of the gleaming maple floor, the whole thing was magical, the elegance and skill was just sublime. After dancing the standard ballroom dances they finished off with a delightful Charleston routine both dressed in stripped suits with boaters and canes. Following the standing ovation Peter said something like "You work on perfecting your Feather Step for thirty bloody years and then they all clap your Charleston." Unforgettable!

A few months later I caught the eye of one of a new crop of RADA girls. Her name was Misty Lake at least that's the name she used. She was a very posh 'mummy and daddy' type, the type who always got what they wanted. She wanted me and although I had tried to steer clear of shagging students since Lenny had warned me it was being noticed and frowned upon I was helpless in the face of temptation. I agreed to go on a date with her. I just hoped no-one at the school would find out. Miss Haylor, called me into her office at The Mardi the following evening and I feared the worst but she just wanted to tell me she was pleased with my progress. The RADA girls had all studied ballet before and they found the footwork in Ballroom hard to grasp, they couldn't keep their toes together either. I knew I was in her good books as soon as I walked in because she called me 'Darling.' This was always a sign that she was pleased with me, if she wasn't it was 'Ducky.' She hadn't found out about Misty. I had a reprieve. She reminded me, as she always did, to dance with Nerina when I went back into the club which I did and enjoyed doing. She was as bad a dancer as Miss Haylor was sublime but the great joy of her company was her humour and kindness. I didn't need reminding. We did a slow Foxtrot. I thanked her and walked her back over to her place at the bar. The Major beckoned me to him and told me it was 'nicely done.' He was drunk. I'd noticed that he had been drunk a lot of the time recently. Drunks are not the greatest of company. You can't trust them. They can turn on you quickly. We'd take turns on the microphone as MC for the evening, three-quarters of an hour each, and when I was on I called Lenny and Doreen Key, his professional partner, onto the floor to give an exhibition of the Cha cha cha to 'Spanish Flea' by Ray McVay. Lenny gave me a raised eyebrow at my cheek but he and Doreen did a rhythm packed, body rippling performance that had the audience up on its feet applauding. I stayed behind with Lenny to carry on drinking after everyone else had gone though he warned me we had to be careful. I was still underage.

By then I had about twenty private pupils and together with my wage from the Mardi I was doing quite well financially. That said I was always on the lookout for a bit of loose change and I got a part time job modelling jeans at the Levi's showroom in Acton. I was showing a new range for the management one day with another model named Louise Barns, a posh girl with a stunning body, when I noticed a well known TV personality sat in the audience. His name was Jimmy Saville a DJ with long blond hair. He was flashy, always wanting to be the centre of attention and making sounds like a demented sea lion whilst puffing away on a big cigar filling the room with smoke. I said hello and exchanged a few banalities. He'd arrived in a big camper van with a double bed in the back and he was outside showing it to some of the younger models. He invited Louise and I to a 'private party' at his London flat that weekend and we accepted but when we were leaving, Louise told me that he had made her feel very uncomfortable and whispered something in her ear which really disturbed her. It was something she couldn't even bring herself to repeat. I wanted to go back and confront him but Louise told me not to. She just wanted to get out of there. Needless to say we didn't go to his party. We attended another party at a house in Rickmansworth instead. Louise had been invited by a friend who was dating a Watford footballer but before then I had the little matter of my date with Misty to look forward to!

I met Misty at a pub in Swiss Cottage on the Thursday evening. It was packed but she'd managed to get some seats outside. I went inside to get us some drinks and unexpectedly spotted Holly, the shop girl I'd met with her friend at The Purple Pussy, at the far side of the bar. I tried to avoid eye contact but she saw me and came over. I hadn't seen her since that night but she'd phoned the studio several times. I didn't return her calls. I wasn't that keen on pursuing it to be honest but here she was. I lied that I'd tried to call but there was no answer. She suggested we get a seat outside where Misty was waiting for me. I said I'd rather stay inside because of the gnats. It was all I could think of. I found us seats as far away from the front of the pub as possible then excused myself, saying I needed a pee. I got a half for me and a white wine for Misty and pushed my way through the crowded bar back outside. I told her I couldn't get served because it was so packed. Then I said I needed the loo, dashed back inside, got a glass of wine for Holly and went and sat with her. I was gasping for breath by this time. I told Holly I had a touch of asthma because of the humid weather. She wanted to go on somewhere but I further lied that I had a lesson later that evening. She said she'd come with me. Time was passing I'd left Misty alone for all but a minute or two since I'd arrived. I told Holly I'd ring her the next day and we'd go for a meal. I was late for the lesson. I had to rush and rush I did. I got outside and told Misty that the place was too crowded and I'd take her somewhere better. We got a taxi to The Purple Pussy.

There was a long queue waiting to get in and Misty was very impressed that Roy the Boy, the massive doorman, just waved us through. I was giving the manager and his wife lessons at the time and that got me special treatment. I got us drinks and on the pretext of emptying my, what Misty must have thought, tiny bladder I asked Max the DJ, a really cool black guy, to play 'Misty' by Johnny Mathis for me in the next slow section. When I got back Misty told me that she was surprised when I asked her out just ten minutes after meeting her. Ignoring the fact that it was she who asked me out I mumbled something about instant attraction and she seemed pleased. 'Misty' came on and she twigged that I'd arranged it. We danced up close and started necking. A few slow dances later she said she wanted to go back to my place. A taxi ride, a flight of stairs and a key in a door later we were doing the eternal waltz on my white sheets. It was fine but there was a certain desperation about her that unnerved me a little. Still …

Louise picked me up at my digs that Saturday lunchtime and we drove to Rickmansworth in her flower power Morris Minor. The 'house' was in fact a mansion. The Avenue it was in was lined with majestic trees and other mansions.

It was millionaire's row. There was a long shingle driveway which was packed with luxury cars. Both front doors were wide open. A large chandelier hung from the ceiling above the entrance hall and two immaculate waiters with trays of Champagne stood at the foot of a sweeping staircase leading up to a galleried landing. 'Crocodile Rock' was blasting out through huge but discreet speakers. We took a glass of bubbly each and walked into a room off to the right. The first thing we realised was that 'Crocodile Rock' was not on a record but that there in front of us, sat at a Grand Piano was Elton John himself playing live! It was hard to take in… Elton John sat there in the flesh. He had strong connections with Watford FC at the time and was there with the players for whom the party was being thrown. This was the big league. There were famous music and TV personalities everywhere you looked. As the night wore on the magnificent house became an arena of unbridled sensuality. People were at it everywhere, in the garden, in the swimming pool, on the stairs, on the piano, everywhere. There were no inhibitions. It was a full on Roman orgy. I half expected Julius Caesar to turn up. No-one seemed surprised by this turn of events. On the contrary it was clear that this was the main attraction of the night. They were old hands at it. It's what they'd gone there for. Though mesmerising it was a step too far for us. We observed but did not partake. We weren't that sophisticated. I noticed that Elton John was nowhere to be seen he must have left earlier. Nonetheless it was a party I'd never forget. Louise drove us back to London as dawn was breaking. I'd drunk loads of Champagne and could hardly stand. When we got to Niton Street she had to help me up to my room at 6 am. I had to teach in three hours. Louise made us coffee while I collapsed on the bed. She said she'd stay and drive me into work then she slipped out of her yellow dress and got into bed with me. I still hadn't had a second's sleep when I got into work.

Despite what I'd said I didn't contact Holly for that dinner. I was a right bastard looking back on it. I have no excuses. Soon after, Miss Haylor suggested that Marion Brown, my fellow teacher, book some lessons with me so that I could partner her at her fellowship exams with the ISTD. She was a great dancer and passed the exams with honours. I took her out to a French restaurant afterwards to celebrate. We became good friends. Miss Haylor was pleased. I had recovered from my disastrous marriage by now and everything was back on track ... so I thought! The next day I was taking a Tango lesson for mature learners in the Mardi when Misty turned up. She said she wanted to talk to me and sat and waited until the lesson finished. She accused me of 'seeing' someone else. I explained that though we were friends I didn't regard our relationship as exclusive. We could date but I was a free spirit. That wasn't enough for her. She started crying. I tried my best to comfort her but I was no good in that situation. Then she informed me that she was pregnant. I was dumbstruck. I spluttered out some words but they weren't being said by me. Misty told me that her father knew all about our 'relationship' and that he would literally kill me when he found out. She was his little girl. She was frightened. I told her not to tell him, a smart tactic in the situation. She agreed and we went back to my digs after the last lesson of the day to figure things out. She said that we should get married. I had to tell her then that I was already married, technically and she went into another state of panic. I calmed her by saying that it was easy enough to get a divorce and if necessary I would. She told me that she loved me and wanted us to marry. She said she wanted to spend the rest of her life with me. I was trapped. We lay on the bed and despite the situation one thing led to another and ... well you know.

Later that night Louise turned up. In all the horror and

confusion I'd forgotten she'd said she was going to come round. She let herself in with a key I'd had cut for her and sneaked in to surprise me and found me with Misty entangled, asleep on the bed. I was unaware of this at the time of course but it must've been horrible I suppose. She fled the scene bumping into Mr Mickalov on the way out. Seeing her obvious distress he asked what was wrong but she didn't answer. The next day Mr Mickalov, who knew Louise from her previous visits, told me what he'd seen, her coming down the stairs in a terrible state, rushing out in tears … I realised what must have happened and was really concerned. I dashed around to her flat to try to explain but when I rang the bell there was no answer. I called her name but there was still no response. I knew something was wrong. I broke down the door and found her sprawled on her bed, still dressed, with several empty pill bottles strewn across the floor. Oh God! I dialled 999 and an ambulance rushed her to Kensington Hospital. She survived but was on a drip for over a week. It was all such a shock. Louise was such a sensible person. I'd never have expected her to be capable of doing something like that. For the first time in my life I felt guilt. Things should be simple but that wasn't always the case. I was getting caught up in reality and I didn't like it. I talked to Louise when she was out of the hospital and she told me that it wasn't just finding me in bed with Misty that made her take the pills. It was a whole load of things. She felt ridiculous for having done it. I told her about the situation with Misty and that I cared about her and would never have done anything to hurt her on purpose. She said she understood and we agreed to remain good friends. That was one thing that turned out all right at least. One thing less to play on my conscience!

I confided in Lenny over lunch in Da Benito, an Italian restaurant in Mayfair. I laid it all out on the line, the whole nightmare, Misty's pregnancy, her demand that we get married, me explaining that I was already married, her parents anger, Louise's attempted suicide, my guilt, all of it. Lenny was not sympathetic. He basically told me that I was a stupid little arsehole; that I'd been playing around with people's emotions without regard to their feelings and that always ended badly. I found it hard to argue. He told me to face up to the situation and do what was right. I was feeling bad but I still had something else I needed to confide in him about. I don't know why, it may have had something, or a lot, to do with my complicated personal life but I'd stopped enjoying working at the Mardi. I told Lenny that I was considering a change. He assured me that that could well be a frying pan fire scenario and I should think long and hard before doing anything about it. There were hundreds of dance teachers who would kill their mother to be in my position. It was true but I couldn't shake a growing feeling of discontent. I didn't want to let Miss Haylor down though and I agreed to take things slowly. That said I'd already made an appointment to see Sydney Francis, who ran The Hendon Dance Centre in North London with his long term dance and business partner Anne Gainsmead, the following day. I'd heard that they were looking for a new manager. Lenny's advice was good but I'd keep the appointment anyway. I left Lenny at the bar and went home to get an early night.

The Hendon was situated above a cinema like the Dance Studio in Hadleigh. It had a maple floor, orange lamps in each window, very large mirrors, a small tea bar just inside the ballroom entrance and a small stage at the far end next to a pay phone booth. Sydney Francis greeted me warmly. He was a refined, good looking man with an air of unforced confidence. We sat and he told me that he was looking for a manager to look after the studio because he was away a lot teaching abroad. I said I was definitely interested then he excused himself to answer a call on the payphone. He spoke in muffled tones and seemed a little angry but was fine when he returned to our interview. Five minutes later a pupil, a girl named Daisy, turned up. She was effusing over Sydney like a schoolgirl with a crush which is what she, in fact, was. Sydney shooed her away to wait in reception. He said she got on his nerves but that was the price to pay for being a dance teacher right. I could only agree. He was aware that I had reservations about leaving Miss Haylor which he understood. He knew and liked her. He then confided that he wanted the new manager, whoever that may be, to keep his partner Anne Gainsmead happy when he was on his travels and so forth. She was possessive, paranoid about his activities and he found it wearisome. I said that would be easy enough … probably and then I heard the front door open followed by footsteps on the wooden stairs and the lady herself appeared. She was a blowsy blond in her forties, about five feet tall and very well dressed. She hadn't known about my interview and made it clear that it was for a job that Sydney should be doing himself. There was obvious friction between them. He told her who I was and what experience I had but she brushed that aside and wanted to see if I could dance. As she was putting 'My Cherie' by Al Martino on the record deck Sydney whispered that all she ever wanted was to dance. I was getting the picture. We did a waltz, a Cha Cha Cha, a rumba and then a jive. Both Sidney and Anne were suitably impressed. Sydney took me into his office to discuss things further while Anne stayed to chat with the newly arrived David Douglas, a very well known dance champion, and a couple he was giving lessons to in the ballroom. Daisy was waiting impatiently as we passed. She was nearly two hours early for her session. She flashed her eyes at Sidney who looked at me and gave a 'what can a guy do' shrug. In the office Sydney lit up a large cigar while I had a fag. He offered me thirty quid a week to manage the studio and office. Any private lessons would be split fifty-fifty. It was a good deal, we shook hands on it. He said that I could call him Syd. I told him that I had to go back and talk to Miss Haylor first and I was not looking forward to it. He told me to take my time and ring him when I was ready. I passed Anne on the way out and told her I'd been offered the job. She didn't seem over the moon.

I went back to The Mardi, Miss Haylor was in the Studio with a couple giving a private lesson so I joined Lenny who was having a drink at the bar until she was free. I told him I'd been offered the job and had said yes. He shook his head and said I was being a fool. He could have been right. I sat and pondered the situation. I wasn't happy about telling Miss Haylor. She'd been so good to me, like a mother. I was betraying her. I saw the couple leave and Miss Haylor go into her office. I knocked the door and entered. She wanted to see me anyway. She'd booked me in with a new couple for private lessons the following morning. He was a brain surgeon. She told me that I had to be punctual. My lax timekeeping was becoming an embarrassment. I said I wouldn't be late again and she said I'd better mean it this time. She called me Ducky. I couldn't do it, tell her I was leaving. I just couldn't. That evening Lenny asked me what Miss Haylor's reaction had been and I explained that I'd had second thoughts. I said I'd ring Sydney to let him know. Lenny grinned. His counsel had held sway. He liked being right.

A few weeks later I was driving along Putney High Street in my red Mini with Misty in the passenger seat when my wheels locked, breaking at traffic lights and I slammed into the back of a Jaguar. Other than shock I was fine but Misty hit her head hard against the windscreen and her knees on the dashboard. An ambulance arrived and took her to Putney Hospital. I rode along. I was desperately worried for the baby's sake. After examining her, the doctor told me she was suffering from a mild concussion and some superficial bruising. I asked if the baby was unharmed but he hadn't realised that she was pregnant and immediately called for someone from obstetrics to attend. He asked for Misty's parents contact details to inform them she was there. I pleaded with him not to tell them about the pregnancy as they were unaware of it. He said that could be dealt with another time but he had to let them know about the accident. I sat outside the room with a coffee while they investigated further. I was getting really worried by then. I had never met her parents. They'd be turning up and ... oh shit! I was panicking. I phoned Lenny to come and give me moral support. He said he was on his way. The doctors came out of the room shortly after and I asked if the baby was all right. The first doctor told me that Misty wanted to talk to me so I went in. She was sitting up in the bed and it was obvious she'd been crying. She said she was sorry about the baby and I told her not to be so silly. I was the one who should be sorry. I was driving. If it was anyone's fault it was mine. She said that she didn't mean that. There was no baby, there never had been. She'd made it all up. She asked me to forgive her. She said we could still get married and have lots of babies. These last weeks had been the happiest of her life. She loved me and she knew that I loved her. She said we were made for each other. Her parents didn't know a thing about me either, that was another lie. It was all an elaborate plan to trick me into marriage. It was happening again! Was this to be the pattern for the rest of my life, being an unwilling pawn in the games of romantically obsessed women? I felt such a chump. I told her that she needed to see a psychiatrist, which I believe she actually did a short time later, and then I got out of there as quickly as I could. Lenny turned up and I told him what had happened. The sun had come out. He drove me back to The Mardi in his Triumph Herald Convertible with the roof down; a welcome breeze blew through my hair. I'd had a narrow escape but at least it was an escape. Back at The Studio I phoned Holly and asked her if she wanted to go clubbing that night. She did! We danced, we got drunk and we went to bed. Being a self centred little shit wasn't the worst thing in the world after all. People use each other all the time for all kinds of reasons. Sometimes you are the user and sometimes you are the used. Usually it's benign but sometimes it gets out of hand. It was a lesson I was beginning to learn but I hadn't learned it yet.

Chapter 5

'Tears of a Clown'

It was a quiet afternoon in the Mardi with only Elsa and yours truly present. I was studying the ballroom technique book while waiting to have a lesson with Miss Haylor at 4PM. When Elsa's 3PM phoned in to say they were running late she asked me if I would like to dance a waltz. I threw the book down ready to go. She put a record on the gramophone, I took hold and we began, though over fifty years old she was in incredible physical condition, strikingly beautiful, dressed in her black trousers and blouse with Cuban heeled shoes she looked like Marlene Dietrich, and a wonderful dancer. I'd seen her in action many times and decided to go for gold, double reverse spin, over-spin, throwaway over-sway; continuous natural pivots and so on, the complete works. I was supplying a very strong lead but treating her with adequate respect. All was going well when suddenly without a word Elsa changed hold and took the lead. I was now the lady and she was the man. She stepped it up a notch or two. It was now relentless. Everything was syncopated, I was doing endless heal turns, same foot lunge, travelling contra checks, you name it she produced it! The music ended and she spun me under her arm to finish. I was speechless but not Elsa. She said 'Excellent. Next time you can wear high heels!' We laughed as I became one of her victims. No audience, just for fun, another unforgettable moment of magic for me.

Elsa's couple turned up late for their lesson. Miss Haylor was spot on time for mine. Other teachers, including Michael Houseman and Marion Brown, arrived to take their classes and the place was abuzz until we wound up around eight. Elsa and I retired to the bar behind the curtains for a swift one before the beginning of the usual evening social. It was a day off for Lenny and the Major was doing the necessaries in his absence. Our jokes were not appreciated. The Major had no time for either levity or smut and when I asked for a Vodka and lime on the rocks he dismissed my request with an offhand 'You must be joking boy!' I was livid but decided not to make a fuss. Elsa and I went to nearby pub instead where the atmosphere was more laissez faire but a few weeks later I had a major falling out with the Major.

It must be said that I wasn't in a very good mood to start with. I'd just finished giving a class and I'd not enjoyed it. I was furious at myself for not being at my best and I put it down to my ongoing discontent with the job. I went into the club for a drink. The Major was behind the bar and he made an unwarranted wisecrack about my punctuality. I ignored it and asked for a vodka and lime. He told me I was underage and, as on the previous occasion, he wasn't going to serve me. I said that Lenny had no problem with it nor did Miss Haylor. The Major said that was their business but he wouldn't serve me full stop. I became angry and told him that he was a pain in the arse and that no-one in the place liked him. I demanded he serve me. Now getting redder and redder in the face he replied that I was an ungrateful little whippersnapper and it was he who had got me my job there in the first place. Then he fired me on the spot. I told him that he could stick his job where the sun don't shine and stormed out.

Lenny stopped me in the ballroom and asked what the hell all the shouting was about. I told him I'd been fired and he said that I should take no notice of what the Major said as he was in no position to fire anyone. Only Miss Haylor could do that. She was on holiday in Malta with Nerina at the time but he was sure she'd sort it all out when she got back. I told him that I was finished with the Mardi anyway and I was going to phone Sydney Francis to see if the job offer was still there. I'd had enough. It was a relief to get out into the coolness of the night. I could breathe again. The following morning I phoned Sydney and got the Hendon job.

A few days later Miss Haylor got back from her holiday and was devastated when Lenny told her the news. She asked to see me and I went to her office. I explained what had happened with the Major and she said that, as Lenny had assured me, he was in no position to sack me or anyone else. She told me I should forget about it and carry on as normal but I replied that it was too late as I'd already got another position. She was visibly shocked but seeing that my mind was made up she wished me luck anyway. She said that I'd always know where she was if I needed her. I kissed her on the cheek and left the office in tears. Miss Haylor was very upset too and immediately called the Major in. I heard their conversation through the open door. She said that I had character and spirit and was a great asset to the studio and that his foolish pride had thrown it all away. He tried to defend himself but was no match for Miss Haylor who tore a strip off him in no uncertain manner. I felt sorry for the chap.

Thinking about it in the cold light of day I realised that the unpleasant interchange I'd had with the major was more my fault than his. I was in a bad mood and as soon as I saw him at the bar I knew that he wasn't going to serve me. I should have just left but I didn't. I was spoiling for a fight, some sort of catharsis and I used the Major's predictability to create it. The truth was that he had a valid point. I was underage and he could have got into trouble if he'd been caught serving me alcohol. I'd just got used to Lenny doing it but that didn't make it right or acceptable. The Mardi could have lost its license. I was addressing an elder and well respected figure in the dance world too and though we didn't get on personally I should have had more respect for his position. I was acting like a child. I was not proud of it.

I started at the Hendon the following Monday after having found a new bedsit above a Greek restaurant dead opposite Golders Green tube station, not five minutes away. It was unexpectedly sad leaving Niton Street and Mr Mickalov. He gave me a farewell present. It was an alarm clock with an extra loud alarm. He'd certainly got to know me. We hugged and said goodbye. The new place was roomier than Niton Street and sparsely but nicely furnished with a large double bed and a duvet. I shared a bathroom with the restaurant chefs though I rarely saw any of them in there. I assumed that they never went to the toilet or washed their hands. The rent was ten quid a week and that included a meal every evening in the restaurant. It was Greek food of course which was new to me. I got to like it a lot. Some nights I'd get home late, in the early hours, and then I'd go to the all night Wimpey bar next to the station opposite for a mixed grill. I'd sit there for a while chilling out watching the young couples and the sad loners at the other tables. It was kind of romantic.

The curtains in my bedsit didn't reach together properly and the room was illuminated at night by the orange light of the Wimpey sign flickering across the ceiling. I'd lie there half asleep waiting for the occasional car to creep past, wondering who was in it, where had they been, where were they going. London in the dead of night has a hollow, melancholy beauty to it. It becomes a City of Dreams.

Within a few weeks of starting at the Hendon I received a phone call from Patric Plumb, the world renowned dance specialist who ran the Regency Dance Centre in Wimbledon. He'd found out that I'd finished at the Mardi and moved to the Hendon and he told me that he could make me a much better offer to join him instead. I informed Sydney about it and he was disappointed. He thought I was happy at the Hendon and I was but I wanted to get as much experience as I could. I wanted to absorb knowledge. He warned me that this sort of flitting from job to job would gain me a reputation as being a fly by night. He was probably right but I went to see Patric Plumb nonetheless.

Patric Plumb AKA 'The Duchess of Wimbledon' answered the door at the Regency dressed in a frilled lilac shirt with several gold chains around his neck, a selection of Diamond rings on his fingers and smelling strongly of Aramis aftershave. He introduced himself, welcomed me in and led me through the Regency Ballroom, one of the three studios, into his office. There was a small bar just inside the door and a single bed against the back wall. He offered me a drink and seeing the time of day I said I'd have a tea or coffee. Ignoring this he picked up a crystal glass, put in some ice cubes and asked 'Whiskey, Gin, Vodka or Brandy!' It was clear he was not related to the Major. I joined him in a G&T, he took a small white pill with his, and we sat and talked. I asked him about the pill and he said it was nothing, just his medication. I forgot about it. He told me that he was looking for a manager to take the pressure off him as he wasn't feeling too well of late. I assured him it was a job I was well capable of doing and he said he didn't doubt for a moment. The phone rang and he answered it. It was a woman asking him if he was available to judge a dance competition on a Sunday the following month. He checked his diary and saw that he had a prior engagement then, putting his hand over the mouthpiece, asked if I was free on that date. I told him I had several private pupils booked but he waved his hand dismissively and replied that I had plenty of time to cancel them. I protested that the pupils wouldn't be happy about that and he said 'Fuck 'em. Tell them to dance in the competition you'll be judging.' He told the woman on the phone that he couldn't do it but she could have me, George Lloyd, his new manager, to sit on the panel in his stead. She was evidently happy with that. Patric bade her farewell and hung up. 'There we are you're booked to judge for Bill and Sylvia Mitchell at the Rivoli Ballroom three weeks this Sunday!' I didn't know what to say. He poured me another G&T and announced that I could start at the Regency the following Monday. I thanked him but said I'd have to speak to Sydney first out of respect at which he did the most remarkable thing. He stood up dramatically, put his left hand on his hip, raised the right above his head, stamped his foot down hard on the floor, like a matador in a bullring, and bawled out 'Sydney!! Sydney Who! Remember you're in Regency now Darling. The Duchess has spoken!' I laughed out loud. He warmed to his performance and continued 'As for his old friend from Balham – Nina Hunt, there's a cold wind blowing from Balham High Road' and raising his glass high above his head he toasted 'I'd rather have the cream on Wimbledon Broadway than the sour milk on Balham High Road!' I'd heard of Nina Hunt of course, she was a legendary teacher of Latin dance, but other than that I didn't have the faintest idea what he was on about. It was clear however that Patric Plumb was no ordinary man. Before I left he instructed me to pick him up from his flat at Tymperley Court, Wimbledon Common, on Monday morning at ten thirty sharp. I said I'd be there.

I talked to Sydney and he agreed that I could split my week between the Hendon and the Regency. Patric was okay with this too so a happy compromise was reached. I'd get the experience, knowledge and inspiration from both. I didn't realise it at the time but they were not the closest of friends as Sydney was in cahoots with Nina Hunt, Patric's arch enemy, and it was rare that the two men would agree on anything. Patric's bizarre poetic outburst at our first meeting made sense when I learned of this. I had met quite a few gay men in the dance world by that time but Patric was different. He would say and do the most outrageous things regardless of where he was and who was present. He was literally shameless. I've seen him walk into a crowded roomful of strangers, strike up a theatrical pose and declaim 'God has arrived!' in an ear shattering camp tenor voice that would stun the place into silence and then proceed to hold court like a renaissance king among his subjects, hypnotising them with his oblique charm on more than one occasion. He was the sun around which the planets revolved.

Back at the Hendon things carried on as normal but it became increasingly clear to me that 'normal' was not an ideal state. It wasn't the work, that was fine, excellent in fact but the relationship between Sydney and Anne was often painful to observe. They weren't an item as I had originally thought but Anne desperately wanted them to be. She was a wealthy widow and had fallen head over heels for Sydney for whom she bought and financed the dance school. Her money kept the place afloat when business wasn't booming too. She did all this so as to be close to him. He appreciated it but his appreciation wasn't going to stop him pursuing his great loves, travel and casual sex, twin knives in Anne's heart. She wanted him near and hers. Sydney wasn't subtle about his proclivities either. I actually interrupted him mid action in his office on more than one occasion. Anne would be aware of what was going on and be in despair. 'Did you see that? He's gone into the office with one of his floosies, right in front of me. He doesn't care.' I'd dance with her to take her mind off things. Sydney himself would deny that anything was going on and put it down to Anne's paranoia whilst at the same time thanking me for 'keeping her busy!' All she wanted was to dance with Sydney and be his love but that was a pipe dream. It was difficult not to come to the conclusion that Sydney's overriding interest in Anne was a financial one and that at heart Anne knew it. Being toyed with in this careless and somewhat cruel manner was a price she was prepared to pay just to be near him. I didn't like being in the middle of this tragic scenario and after a time I made this clear to Sydney and my 'keeping her busy' phase came to an end.

I was there at Tymperley Court ten thirty on the dot. I rang the bell and Patric called out 'Push the door, it's on the latch.' I went in and the same voice called from the bedroom 'Take a seat. I'm nearly ready.' The flat was filled with lavish antiques, lamps and crystal, and the walls were covered in gilt framed paintings and photographs. I could hear Patric talking gently from within the bedroom 'Right mum, I'm off now. Your lunch is all done. See you later my love.' He came into the living room leaving the door ajar behind him and explained 'My mum, she's getting old now bless her.' There was a matching gilt edged onyx cigarette box and lighter on one of the small tables, he offered me a cigarette and lit it for me. I told him I'd been admiring his antiques and he replied that it was his passion, that he just couldn't stop buying them 'If I see something I like I've just got to have it!' He was looking at me as he spoke and I thought I detected a hint of subtext but he saw this, smiled and said 'Not you love. I don't do straight guys and I've got my Alan.' I breathed a little sigh of relief. Patric donned his camel hair overcoat, draped his gold satin scarf around his neck and we departed for the Regency. We drove there in my famous red mini and on the way he invited me to go with him to visit a dear friend of his in Bayswater on the Friday afternoon. He said she was an important person to get to know. I was happy to accept.

Patric's first couple arrived for their lesson. They were adult amateurs. Patric put on a Rumba, 'Love is Blue' and they began their routine. Things seemed to be going nicely when the music suddenly stopped. Patric screamed at the man 'For Christ's sake, when you do that line you need to keep your bloody balls off the floor!' then he grabbed the lady by the arm and demonstrated. 'Look I'll show you, like this. 2341, 2341 and lunge 2341, extend, keep your back-side in and your balls off the floor!' I was startled by this teaching method but the couple took it in their stride and carried on laughing and enjoying the lesson. My first pupils arrived a short time later. They were about the same age as Patric's couple and also adult amateur status. Both lessons continued simultaneously. My couple were doing a Rumba too. I put on 'Spanish Eyes' by Al Martino and walked among them offering small adjustments of posture and shape where necessary. Patric poured himself a large G&T and lit a cigarette as he watched on from the sidelines shouting out suggestions and insults in equal measure. The couples loved it and thanked both Patric and myself profusely before leaving together. Ten minutes later the doorbell rang again. It was Bill and Sylvia Mitchell. They said that they were really looking forward to having me judge for them at the Rivoli. I thanked them and went to get Patric who'd retired to his office. I knocked the door but there was no answer. I knocked again then opened it tentatively to see him lying asleep on the bed. I woke him gently and told him his next lesson had arrived but he said that he wasn't feeling well and that I should take it. I left, shut the door behind me and explained the situation to Bill and Sylvia who were happy to continue with me. They had been working on a Rumba routine with Patric and we picked up on it. I put on 'Strangers in the Night' and they showed me their ten bar opening. It was nicely choreographed. We carried on from there and things flowed and sparked with natural ease. From that night on I became their regular teacher and we became good friends.

We visited Patric's 'dear friend' in Bayswater on the Friday afternoon as arranged and I was delighted to find it was none other than Elsa Wells my old sparring partner from the Mardi. The mystery of how Patric found out I'd left so soon was solved. Patric knew we were friends of course and the subterfuge was for the surprise element. The flat was even more luxurious than Patric's and Elsa's hospitality was second to none. In fact with G&T's flowing the evening, as it did on our many subsequent evenings in Bayswater, quickly degenerated into being every bit as filthy and funny as Elsa, Lenny and I had been in the Mardi. I can remember the stories and the laughter so well. They just treated me as one of them. It was incredibly entertaining and it also gave me a further insight into the world of Ballroom dancing. I was flattered that they trusted me, they certainly didn't hold back, however I always kept the content of our conversations private. After all it wouldn't be politic telling another professional male dancer that Elsa Wells thinks that he's a conceited idiot and that he reminds her of Max Wall would it.

The Rivoli was packed to the rafters with dance enthusiasts, relatives and friends as the first competition for the juvenile and junior ballroom got under way. It was a good standard and enjoyable to watch. They were followed by the Adults Novice, Pre-Amateur and then Amateur. There were some excellent dancers in all categories and a fantastic atmosphere but later some of the parents didn't look too happy and could be seen whispering to each other about why their children didn't make the final. I would hopefully be picking up some more private lessons. The final dance of the competition was a Jive to 'Rock Around The Clock'. The audience were tapping their feet in their seats and clapping in time to the music then when it finished they rose as one, applauding and cheering the roof off. The atmosphere was electric. Bill announced that we, the judges, would now take our time to deliberate and that the floor was open to all. Couples stampeded onto the dance area as the opening bars of 'Ruby Don't Take Your Love to Town.' filled the air. It was their time to strut their stuff and they did so with unleashed gusto. Gordon Fletcher, one of the other two judges, asked me to judge the West Midland Championships which he was running in Worcester a few weeks later. I checked my diary and I was free so the date was booked then Stan Page, the other judge, asked me to check out the 28th of November when he had a big competition in Birmingham and though I had a few private lessons I knew I could rearrange them so I booked that too. Sylvia Mitchel grabbed me for some future dates there at the Rivoli as well. I was being inundated with judging work. I wondered aloud if my fee was too low and everybody laughed. I meant it though. At the results and prizes presentation Bill praised the overall standard of the competitors and announced that making his debut at the Rivoli, one of the evening's judges and a very good friend of his, George Lloyd would be making the presentations. I returned to the floor to huge applause and as the couples were called up to receive their prizes they all had their photos taken with me, looking very cool in my grey mohair suit. Afterwards some of the winning couples asked me for my autograph, whereas most of the losers were looking at me sideways.

Chapter 6

'That's Life'

The next day, tired but elated from the night before, I turned up for my scheduled lessons at the Regency uncharacteristically on time. Patric turned up late in a taxi. He'd been to the doctors. Things seemed fine at first but when my couple left he came at me like a wildcat. He was furious at the marks I'd given 'his' couples at the Rivoli, I'd put them second, third and fourth. He screamed that I was a swine and my job was to mark his dancers first. I told him I'd been fair and marked as I saw it but that infuriated him even further. He told me not to go crying to him when my lesson diary was empty and then implied that I had no doubt been 'into the knickers' of the girl of the winning couple. I told him I took offence at that and he replied that he 'didn't give a fuck' then stormed off to have a lie down before his first pupils arrived 'If they turn up at all after the fucking marks you gave them!' I was both annoyed and disappointed though over the years I have learned that such chicanery was essentially the norm in the world of dance competition. I am no saint as you are aware but I just couldn't go along with it. Dance training requires such hard work and commitment, my admiration and respect for those who compete made me determined to mark with fairness and an open mind, as I had done that first night at the Rivoli, and to this day I have never done otherwise. It has turned some people in the dance community against me but to quote my esteemed mentor 'Fuck 'em!'

When Patric's first couple arrived he breezed out of his office as if he didn't have a care in the world. He was charm itself. Such was the enigmatic nature of the man. One thing though, the affectionate nickname 'Swine' stuck, which delighted me. Well you all know how much I love pigs right!

One thing about all this, most dance competitions judges were much older than me, this was the norm. The fact that I was only nineteen did raise a few eyebrows among them, however with the backing of Miss Haylor, Elsa, Bill, Sydney and of course the infamous Patric, rightly or wrongly the rules and regulations were overlooked in my case and nobody ever queried it. I was in constant demand though my schedule wasn't exclusively taken up by judging.

I first met Sandra Homans at the Hendon Dance Centre along with her friends Ten Dance Champions Gary Richardson and Sue Pedvin. Sandra was also a very accomplished dancer with years of experience competing in competitions. Sydney Francis and Patric had brought us together with the aim of getting me to partner her and compete as a professional. I found the prospect terrifying. It was something I had never had any desire to do but I suppose there must have been a kind of curiosity lurking within me and under Sydney and Patric's relentless persuasion I finally caved in and agreed. The first step was getting the dance routines together, lots of practice, endless sweat and effort, then down to the tailor, Ron Gunn in Leyton, East London to be measured for my tail suit and cat suit. At the time the traditional cat suit was made with sleeves in jacket form and sleeveless cat suits, though more comfortable, were only worn for demonstrations. However I decided to be a trail blazer from the start and opted for the sleeveless to wear when competing. It certainly got me noticed and undoubtedly cost us votes with some old school judges.

In 1974 we entered for the British and International Professional Ballroom and Latin Championships in Blackpool and the Royal Albert Hall. We were competing against seasoned professionals at the top of their game, couples like the superb Latin Champions, Michael Stylianos & Lorna Lee and Ballroom Royals, Richard & Janet Gleave, the crème de la crème of the dance world. Can you imagine it? I was thrilled and humbled to be in such illustrious company. When we arrived at the Albert Hall I trotted along behind the 'Duchess' dutifully carrying his bag which contained a bottle of gin, two crystal glasses and several bottles of tonic water. He was splendidly attired as usual at such events, dripping in gold jewellery and wearing a gold lamee suit, gold lamee shirt, gold lamee bow tie and golden boots with a camel hair coat thrown casually over his shoulders. He looked like a Glitter Ball on legs. As we entered the building he informed the doorman that, 'God has arrived!' then indicating me 'This is my road manager and those' pointing to the bag, 'are my shoes'. Then flouncing through the lobby he spotted his hated rival, Latin specialist Nina Hunt, with a small group of acolytes. She was wearing a long dress with a target design print and Patric made a big thing of stopping, looking her up and down and saying 'You always look lovely in that dress dear.' He was an awful man but my god was he funny.

Just before going onto the floor I noticed Queen of Latin, Doris Lavelle, giving me the evil eye due to my attire. She had made it clear that sleeveless cat suits could never be worn in competitions. It was gospel to her but I was young and rebellious. I wanted to be different, to stand out. We made our way across the floor and danced the first twelve bars of Basic Rumba right in front of her face. There were also Syncopated Horse and Carts and Pot Stirrers going off everywhere. The Horse and Cart was a move where the girl ran on the spot forwards or backwards at great speed while the boy held one hand around her waist swivelling on one leg with the other leg extended. The Pot Stirrer was a move where the girl crouched down on one foot with the other leg extended to the side and slightly bent at the knee, right arm straight up above the head while the boy rotates her with his right hand as fast as he can. Every dancer did these crowd pleasing moves at the time but they have since become extinct. Doris Lavelle hated every aspect of them. Basic Rumba was her passion, and at least she marked us through to the second round. Of course eventually, several years later, after I had broken the taboo, everyone changed to sleeveless cat suits but that was too late to save me. I had behaved like a stupid brat but at that age what could people expect. I hadn't wanted to get involved in that type of competition in the first place and now here I was dancing in front of hardened championship adjudicators who were openly hostile from the off. They made it clear they didn't give a damn who I was or where I had suddenly sprung from. I could taste the contempt in the air. I could see it in their eyes. 'Who does this little shit think he is? Does he really think we will be impressed by a skinny runt doing a dance routine in a pantomime cat suit?' I smiled and got on with it. Our performance was fine, well it was fine as far as the audience reaction was concerned but the mood from the judging panel was icy cold. You'd think I was in a courtroom on trial for killing my mother. It was becoming clear to me what you'd have to do to please these people. You'd have to toe the line, bite your tongue, have some lessons with various influential judges and not take the piss in a sleeveless cat suit before you'd have any hope of success in their world. Natural talent, lots of practice, hard work and total dedication was, as I feared, not enough. It was nowhere near enough. I was an unwelcome guest at a private party. I did have my supporters in the audience however, Lenny and Doreen, who had won the Championship in 1954, and Marion and Miss Haylor, who was also judging, from The Mardi, John

Irvine and Shirley Day and The Duchess of course, who was busy spreading the word among the other judges, not the best idea he ever had. Another mystery fan, a young professional dancer living in South West London, telephoned me the following day with a bucketful of compliments about my performance. She said I was amazing that she couldn't take her eyes off me and she was lonely by herself in the house. She invited me to spend the afternoon with her. I was flattered by the invitation and I couldn't refuse. The Lloyd magic was undimmed. The competition had ended with spectacular performances on the dance floor. Michael Stylianos and Lorna Lee won for the fifth year running. The battle royal continued between Alan and Hazel Fletcher and Peter Maxwell and Lynn Harman, two fabulous amateur couples at the top of their game who would soon dominate the professional Latin scene.

As the Championship progressed Patric became more and more under the influence of gin and tonic and correspondingly more outrageous. On noticing a Japanese couple among the competitors he proceeded to walk a complete circuit of the dance floor, passing behind his fellow adjudicators, calling out 'Remember Pearl Harbour!' A ripple of disgust ran through the audience like a Mexican wave. It was excruciating. During the drive back to Wimbledon I asked Patric if he thought he'd acted wisely making a scene like that. He replied, 'Fuck em' then fell asleep on the back seat.

Patric was a one off, an immensely talented but complex man, a combination of a heart of gold and at times, brutally unkind wit. There were those who couldn't stand him but the majority of people found him amusing and there was a private kindness that some had experienced which made them forgive, and in many cases, love him. I am one such person. He was unique.

Early alarm, it's a lovely sunny Sunday driving my 1965 Daimler Jaguar Mk 2 on the motorway to Worcester. Just another day judging a championship or so I thought. There were five judges, David Douglas, Bob Barber, Rodney Weeks, Alex Moore MBE (chairman) and myself and it was a great turnout with some very talented dancers. One couple in the junior section were exceptional, Peter Townsend and Alyson Bacon. They won convincingly. I remember thinking how skilled they were, natural rhythm, charisma, all it took to go right to the top. I found myself taken with how beautiful the girl was in her white fringe Latin dress. She was stunning but I pushed the thought to the back of my mind as she was just fourteen years old. At the end of the day as I was leaving the venue, her mother stopped me for a chat, thanking me for my marking. I said I didn't need thanks, her daughter and her partner deserved every point they got. In the following years she would regularly seek me out for a catch up after competitions and I got to look forward to it. I had no idea that this lovely lady would go on to play such a huge part in my future life.

I was invited to judge a dance competition at the Western Studio back in Essex. It was strange going back to my old haunts, the place where it all began, but it was lovely catching up with Bob and Marian. The competition went well and I was pleased for them, that they still attracted such a large and enthusiastic clientele. While there I went to see my mum and dad. Mum had moved in with her new bloke permanently. She seemed the same as ever, no different to how she'd been when she lived with dad. I couldn't understand what she'd achieved by going but it's not possible to see inside someone's heart is it, no matter how close you are or how much you love them. She told me that dad had shut himself away and rarely left the house. I went to visit him and found him asleep in my single bedroom with a half empty bottle of Johnny Walker's next to the bed. As usual the house was immaculate and dad had prepared the main bedroom for me with folded towels on the bed, he could not face sleeping alone in this bed anymore, a lovely aroma coming from the kitchen indicated that he had one of his famous casseroles in the oven. I noticed a crystal whiskey glass on the kitchen worktop and another in the lounge next to dad's armchair. He had always drunk in the pub, never at home apart from Christmas. I sat quietly alone reminiscing and thinking of the happy times we had shared as a family. Eventually dad woke up and came down stairs. He was in a bad way. He'd been ill but he didn't want to go into the details and snapped at me when I tried to press him. Although he denied it I knew that he was lonely. It was awful seeing him like this. He'd always been such a vibrant man, full of fun, full of mischief but the man now before me had no sparkle in his eyes. Instead they were dull and misted from lack of sleep and tears. We shared the delicious casserole together, I noticed his hands shaking, he was making an effort to appear normal and sober to me, but I could see beyond it. I stayed the night, in the morning I was woken by 'Frank Sinatra' bellowing out 'That's Life' on the record player accompanied by the smell of sizzling bacon. I noticed that whiskey bottle was now empty. After breakfast I approached the subject of his health but again he rejected my concerns and simply said "I've had a great life now it's your turn son". He hugged me and wished me a safe journey back to London. I was heartbroken to see him like this but there seemed no way of reaching him so I said my good-byes and left.

I called into the garage at a local supermarket to fill up on petrol for the journey back and while there I saw my old nemesis Mike Scaratt. He was gathering up the discarded grocery trolleys in the car park, linking them together and pushing them in a line back to the bay outside the shop entrance where they were kept for customers to pick up. I watched him from the Daimler. He looked so ... defeated. The Mighty Mike Scaratt, leader of men, punisher of queers, the lord of boot and fist reduced to this, pushing a metallic serpent across a car park. How the mighty had fallen. I caught his eye. The contrast between us, with me sat at the wheel of the Daimler, could not have been starker. We stared at each other for a brief moment then he turned away and I drove off singing Frank Sinatra's 'That's Life'.

My Daimler was in action once again a short while later driving Patric, one of my fellow judges, and scrutineer Joy Weller to the Strawberry Dance Festival in Cambridge. Though we took off in the early morning, Patric, dressed down in a plum coloured dinner jacket, pink frilled shirt, plum velvet bow tie, black trousers and black patent boots and sat in the back with his crystal glass, Gin, tonic and ice bucket, had already started drinking. He was distinctly merry when we arrived at the venue and after he introduced himself in his usual flamboyant manner to the people in the busy reception area, we made our way, somewhat unsteadily, to the judge's changing room. I put on my dark blue evening suit and we went to have a look at the set up. The stage was filled with the trophies to be won and a hundred or so punnets of fresh strawberries. The organisers gave a punnet to every finalist. Joan thought it a lovely idea but Patric was repulsed 'Strawberries give me the shits Love' being his loud and dismissive response. Then he began calling out a chant, a song I suppose you could call it – 'Strawberries, fucking great strawberries!' I decided to water down his gin when he wasn't looking.

When the competition was ready to start Joan Jennings, the co-organiser, welcomed the contestants and introduced the judges including the increasingly more intoxicated Patric who strode forward at the mention of his name and took a deep bow to raucous applause. The competition kicked off with the Waltz, we judges standing around the floor marking the couples as they swept past. It continued with the Tango, the quickstep and the Paso Doble, ending with the jive performed to

'Rock Around the Clock' by Bill Halley and The Comets. The crowd went wild, standing on their feet clapping and cheering when it finished and Joan thanked all the competitors and the audience for making it such a special day. Patric chirped in with 'Even the ones who couldn't dance love!' I asked him to keep his voice down but he just said 'Fuck 'em.' and dragged himself off to check the marks. He sat next to Joy Weller at the scrutineer's table and became increasingly and visibly angrier as he looked over the sheets. He gave me a stare that would stop a clock ticking and cornered me on his way to present the prizes, 'You've fucking done it again to my couples!' I protested that I'd marked them fairly and nothing else but that seemed to enrage him further, 'Fairly! … Fucking fairly!! … You need to make your mind up whose fucking side you are on!!!' I said that I wasn't on anyone's side and Patric sneered that if I wasn't going to be one of his disciples it was my funeral, then he strode over to present the trophies and the strawberries all the time continuing to swill back G&T's like a man dying of thirst. He started to perform again within minutes laughing and singing at the top of his voice 'Strawberries, fucking great strawberries. Come and get 'em! Strawberries, fucking great strawberries!!' Luckily the juniors had all left by this time and only adults were left to receive their prizes. Most people were laughing although some were glaring at him but that didn't deter him one bit. If anything it pushed him on to even greater extremes. He was as drunk as a skunk. When the presentation thankfully came to an end Joan and I half carried, half dragged him out of the building before a lynch mob could be organised. A young adult couple stopped me and asked if I would give them private lessons. I gave them my number and told them to call me the next day. Patric slurred 'Put your money in your piggy banks darlings. If you give it to this swine he'll still mark you last' then as we manhandled him through the exit door he grabbed co organiser Joan Jennings by the shoulders and stage whispered 'Joan, he'll have her knickers off before you can say Strawberries, fucking strawberries!' We got him into the back of the car and drove off at speed. It felt as though we were leaving the scene of a crime. Patric didn't relent though. He carried on shouting and raving about my marking until I said it's been a lovely successful day and my conscience was clear. Patric was bamboozled by this and reverted to singing his strawberry song again until he fell asleep, snoring like a warthog in the back seat. When we got back to London he woke up and it was as if nothing had happened. I helped him out of the car and he thanked me for looking after him, 'See you in the morning, god bless you wee Georgie.' What could I say?

Patric phoned me a few days later and told me he wasn't feeling well and asked if I'd mind driving him to his appointment at the hospital the following morning. The appointment was at ten. I told him I'd pick him up at half nine. I took him to the hospital as arranged. It was the first of what turned out to be many trips. Patric never wanted to talk about his illness and I respected his wishes. It was the same as with my dad. Men in those days disliked sympathy. In most ways you would never have found two men less alike than them but in this they were as one. After this, Patric began to take regular naps in his office in the afternoons and would often ask me to take his later classes when he didn't feel up to it. I'd take them side by side with my own. I didn't mind this. I liked him knowing he could rely on me.

A couple of months after the Strawberry debacle there was a night of competitions, including a Professional Latin American International Team Match, arranged by Patric, at the Regency. It was England versus Australia with Elsa and John Wells and Doris Lavelle judging. Among the couples dancing were: Michael Stylianos and Lorna Lee, Ian and Ruth Walker, with yours truly and Sandra Homans for England then Robert and Helen Richie, Bernard and Jan Reilly, Philip and Jan Nicholas for Australia. I felt a great pride representing my country and even greater pride being on the winning team.

Bolstered by my success I joined up with Barney Conway to run a day of dance competitions at The John Donaldson Dance School in Walthamstow. The studio, which wasn't particularly big, was above a row of shops on the main street. I'd taken the unprecedented step of booking fifteen judges for the event. It was a lovely sunny day and people turned up in their droves. Over a hundred were queuing up outside when another bloody big coach load arrived and another, and …. until eventually there were over three hundred dancers and spectators waiting to get in. The scrutineer pointed out that with fifteen judges involved it would take at least three days to complete the contest but I had promised fifteen and there were going to be fifteen. A system was worked out whereby it could be done in one – just! Another pressing problem was that we didn't have any dressing rooms other than two small toilets we could utilise. I went outside and had a word with the coach drivers who graciously gave us permission to use their coaches for the purpose. Lo and behold we had surmounted the insurmountable. Barney eventually made the announcement to get the party started and invited the junior competitors to the floor for the first heats. He selected 'The Last Waltz' by The Ray McVay Orchestra and put it on the turntable saying 'I thought we might start with 'The Last Waltz' for those of you who don't make it through to the next heat!' The laughter roared through the ballroom and the rest of day went with a real swing.

It was around now I finally accepted that my heart wasn't in competitive dancing and indeed hadn't been from more or less the moment I started it. I had given it a go and enjoyed elements of it but, as I had always thought, it wasn't for me. I decided to hang my sleeveless cat suit up and get on with my true passions, choreography and teaching though Sandra and I continued to give quite a few more demonstrations before our short partnership came to an end. At one point we were contacted out of the blue by the actor Ron Moody to screen test for a TV advert for Marvel Milk. They liked what they saw and we got the job. The ad ran for a long time which resulted in some useful exposure and some very welcome income.

I continued to Judge, lecture and teach, particularly focusing on coaching and creating new choreography from then on, getting to work with, and in some cases befriend, the biggest and best names in the business including Barney Conway, Evelyn Hislop, Tom Walker, John Irvine, Shirley Day, Robin Short, David Douglass, Janice Barb, Ian Walker, Ruth Walker, Sonny Binnick, Michael Stylianos, Lorna lee, Gordon Little, Peter Maxwell, Lynn Harman, Derek and June Green, Pat Woor, Bill Irvine, Bobbie Irvine, Alex Moore, Michael Houseman, Geoffrey Clapham, Pamela McGill, Marion Brown, Nina Hunt, Bobby Short, John Delroy and Len Goodman and many more. I gained particular inspiration from the very talented master of dance John Delroy who lifted my soul with his knowledge and love of the art and Len Goodman who was to later gain fame as a Judge on BBC's Strictly Come Dancing' had always been an inspiration to me, particularly in the early days of my dancing life when he showed off his skills as a great dancer with a sense of humour to match. In the early 70's Len won the "Dual of The Giants" at the Royal Albert Hall. The routine began with the theme music from BBC Sit Com 'Steptoe and Son' and Len made his entrance from behind the spectators meandering down the stairs to the arena dressed in flat clap, neck scarf and rolled up sleeves, basically a rag and bone man, looking around as if he was lost. The audience were in stitches. Then his partner and former wife Cherry Kingston, dressed in a skin tight leotard and high heels, made her entrance to the music of The Stripper. Len soon became interested, stopped fooling around, took her by the hand and danced a stunning routine packed with very difficult lifts.

What started out as a very funny comedy ended with the audience on their feet applauding a truly magical show. I attempted to copy Len's humorous style for a while – but my sense of humour wasn't appreciated by everyone in the dance world and often got me into trouble. Len was unique. He had panache. He could carry it off.

Early one summer's morning I collected Patric from his flat in Wimbledon for a booking to judge a competition at The Bull Ring in Birmingham. My trusty old Daimler had served me well but I had traded it in for a white Ford Zephyr. I got the garage to bolt a pair of gold ballroom dancers from a super dance trophy to the front bonnet which I thought was very classy. Patric thought so too as they complimented his jewellery. He lay back in the soft leather passenger seat like a contented cat. The journey was going well until we got to Spaghetti Junction in Birmingham when steam began to pour from the engine. I wanted to pull over as I thought we were overheating but The Duchess would have none of it ordering me to 'Keep going love, we are nearly there'. I did and a minute or so later the engine exploded and we ground to a halt right at the top of the Junction. I got out to have a look under the bonnet while Patric, in his white suit, bow tie and white boots with his camel hair coat draped over his shoulders, got out, walked to the rear of the vehicle and stuck his thumb out for a lift. He actually managed to flag down a car, containing two junior dance competitors and their parents and as it rolled past me very slowly The Duchess rolled down the window and said 'Don't be too long love. I'll tell them you're on your way.' And off they drove. The breakdown lorry took the car to a storage yard and I managed to get to the venue just in time to judge the first round of dancing in my casual clothes. A few weeks later I had the car collected. It was returned to me minus the gold dancers which, on reflection, I decided not to replace.

It was at times like these when my old friend John Thorpe came to the rescue with his Rumbelows TV van. John was a DJ in an Essex Night Club called Gatsby's. We grew up together and he learnt to dance at The Western. He gave me lifts around the country, Birmingham, Wales, etc. on many occasions, his trusty van never let us down. John was a great DJ and often provided the music at my dance competitions.

The following summer I organised a big competition at The Paddocks on Canvey Island, a large modern ballroom with excellent facilities. There were lots of hand-picked judges including Len Goodman and Cherry Kingston who rounded the evening off with a scintillating demonstration that brought the house down. Once again the place was packed with couples from all over the country. It was a cracking night and The Paddocks became a very popular venue on the back of it. I arranged many more events there which included demonstrations by Bill and Bobby Irvine and Michael Stylianos and Lorna Lee. I also grabbed at an opportunity to do some Latin American practice with the fabulous Pamela McGill when she was between partners. I went on to organise another series of competitions at The Whitehall in Westcliffe on Sea. I was busier than ever, my Daimler ran me from Edinburgh to Brighton and Norwich to Dublin hardly pausing for an MOT but my base remained in London. In 1976 I moved to a flat in Earls Court. I was, what is now referred to as 'upwardly mobile.' I was the Golden Boy!

George with his Dad

George with his Mum

George with his brother Paul

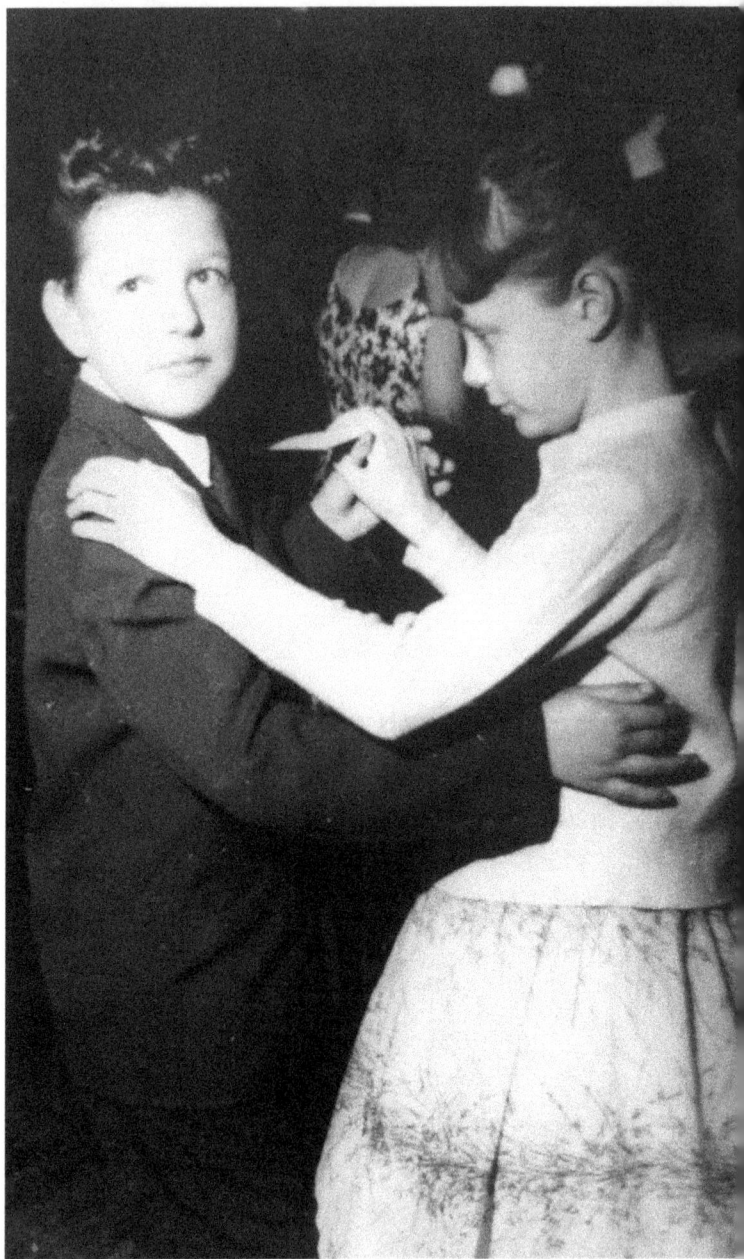

George early dance steps

Bob & Marian Barber

Phyllis Haylor

Peter Eggleton and Brenda

Patric Plumb

George Judging

George with Sandra Homans

Nina Hunt

Rivoli Ballroom London George

George & Alyson Show Dance

Saturday Night Fever

Show Dance

Spain Care Free

Wedding Day

Holiday in Spain

Happy Moments

George & Alyson Carl Alan Awards 1978

Holland Disco Lesson

Disco Show Holland

Holland George & Alyson
Disco Show

Alyson Flying the flag

Team Lloyd Holland

Team Lloyd Ballroom

*Disco Team Ruurd-Klaske
and Michel*

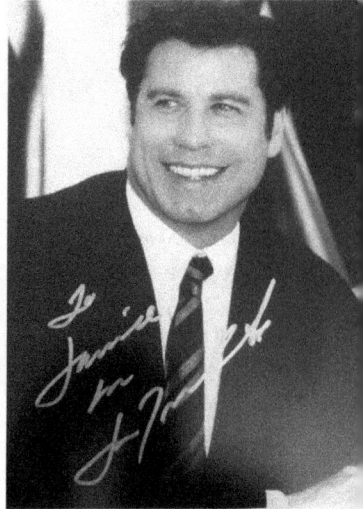

John Travolta

Princess Diana and Jamie

Jamie Molly Lloyd

Larry King CNN

*Rhys Ifans – UNDER MILK
WOOD RUMBA
with Crisian Emanuel*

Our Son Craig Born 12th May 1982

Alyson and George Lunch with Rhys Ifans

Bill & Bobbie Irvine MBE

Sydney Francis

Elsa Wells

Alyson 1981 Holland

Day in the park

Receiving Action Sports Peak Award Holland 1981

Disco Book

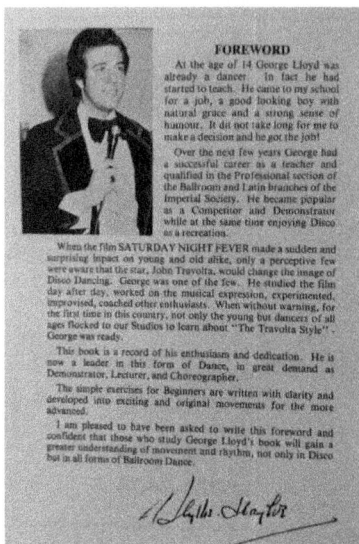

Foreword by Phyllis Haylor

Fever Comp

Teach-in

Lineup

Blue Waters

The author

Chapter 7

'Spirit in the Sky'

I went to The Pussycat for the first time in quite a while. It wasn't a conscious decision not to have gone. I'd been inundated with work and family concerns and time just passed me by. I needed a night on the town to unwind. Roy the Boy greeted me warmly at the door and told me that some of the dancers from Top of The Pops were there. I strutted in to the accompaniment of Boogie Wonderland and headed straight for the dance floor where I got it on with one of the TV professionals, a striking redhead who really knew her stuff. The other dancers loved it and were clapping the beat and cheering our moves. Disco dancing was getting to me. I mean my first love was still ballroom of course but dance is dance, the basic idea, the impetus is the same whatever the style. When the music ended I thanked my partner and went to get a drink. I'd spotted a gorgeous looking girl sat on her own at the far end of the bar and asked Del, the barman, if he knew her. He told me her name was Cherry and she was choosy. All the regular studs had tried their hand but missed out. I asked him to inform her that the handsome dude in the black and white shirt would like to buy her a drink, which he did. She gave me the once over, smiled and said she'd have a Manhattan. I boogied over and joined her. Her full name was Cherry

Popwell … I'll leave it at that! Del had told her I was a professional dancer and she seemed impressed. She was studying law. I said it sounded interesting but she assured me it
wasn't and that she was only doing it to please her father
who was a barrister. I asked her if she wanted to dance and
though she insisted she wasn't very good she joined me on
the floor. She was actually not bad, a natural mover. I told
her so too and suggested she take some 'lessons' with me.
She blushed. I looked at my watch. It was nearly two in the
morning and the club would be closing soon. I asked her if
she'd like to go to the Hendon with me so she could see the
place. I had a key. I promised to drive her home afterwards
and she said OK. When we arrived I took her upstairs to
the ballroom and switched on the lights. She said it was
bigger than she thought it would be. I said nothing. She
walked around looking at the photographs framed on the
wall. She said she liked the look of the place. I turned the
lights down low, switched on the glitter ball and put on a
smoochy record. We danced up close and started kissing
and, well you guessed it, ended up making sweet love on
the lovely sprung maple floor. Afterwards we lay there in the
silence beneath the still turning glitter ball and had a post
coital cigarette. Old Snake Hips had struck again. It was
still the middle of the night when I dropped her home at St
John's Wood. I eventually got to bed at four-thirty. My first
lesson at the studio was booked for nine.

Listen, I am fully aware that this may well make me
sound like a dickhead but the fact is that for that particular
time in my life I was virtually irresistible to the fairer sex. It
was just the way it was. Though passable, I wasn't supernat-
urally handsome but I did have a very fit and lithe body and
dance had taught me how to use it. I was confident too and
didn't mind the occasional knock back. I learned that the
more women you ask to have sex with you the more women

you get to have sex with because they, like we men, also have little else on their minds. I have a belief that in sexual terms every dog has his day and this was mine. Some men miss out altogether in their teens, in their early twenties even, but their day will come. This was my day. I look back on it with interest but none of it was important. It was kids playing. Compared to love it was nothing.

I got a phone call at The Hendon. It was midday and I'd just been into the office to see if Sydney wanted to join Anne and me for lunch. I knocked briefly then entered as I normally did, Sydney had company, he was interviewing an attractive blonde lady. I apologised and made a swift exit but Anne who was waiting outside had got it in her head that Sydney was carrying on with another floozy. I tried to reassure her but she was having none of it. A few minutes later the blonde emerged and scuttled away down the stairs. Anne was furious "Did you see her, half his age. What's he playing at?" Sydney came out of the office, looked at me and just raised his eyebrow at Anne's ranting. I said nothing. I decided to stay out of it. The phone call was from my mother. She told me that my father had had a massive stroke and was in hospital in Southend. I got there as quickly as I could and joined mum in the side room where dad was being treated. He was in a very bad way. He had lost his speech and his arm and leg were paralysed down one side. I said I was glad that she was there with him and she made it clear that just because they no longer lived together it didn't mean she didn't care about him which pleased and comforted me more than I can say. We went into the room. Dad raised his good arm slightly in greeting. I sat on the edge of the bed and kissed him. He had tears in his eyes. I told him that I loved him. I said that everything would be alright. It's strange isn't it that we tell our loved ones this in such circumstances. I had no idea if everything would be alright or not. I feared not but … it's a forlorn attempt at convincing oneself I think. He raised a half smile in response. There were some sheets of writing paper on the top of the blanket and on the bedside cabinet. Mum told me that he'd been trying to write something down all day. I looked at them. It just seemed like scribbling to me but dad reached out to try again. I gave him one of the sheets and a pen. It was painful to watch him struggling to control his hand and body. I looked again and this time I could make out a capital letter D. I asked him if that is what it was and he gave a small nod. He was getting very emotional. It obviously meant a lot to him that I should understand what he was trying to say. I made some suggestions as to what it could represent; drink, doctor, drugs but none of them got a response. A nurse entered and told us Nan had arrived and since they only allowed two visitors at a time I said I'd go and have a word with her then she could take my place. We had a hug and I told her how dad was. I mentioned the writing, the letter D, and told me she thought she knew what it meant. She told me to sit down and said she thought the D stood for daughter. I still didn't understand. Then she informed me that dad had a daughter from a previous marriage. I had a sister. I asked why I'd never been told and she said it just never seemed appropriate and the longer it was left the less important it seemed. Now dad was nearing his end he obviously thought I should know. I was overwhelmed. To hear this on top of dad being so ill was hard to take in. I asked if Nan knew where this sister lived and was even more amazed when she told me she lived in Westcliff which was just up the road from the hospital. She even had her address and she wrote it down for me as I popped back in to the room. Dad had dozed off so I told mum I'd found out about the sister. She said she should have told me but it never seemed to be the right time. There was so much time yet it never seemed the right time. I stroked dad's arm and he stirred. I told him that I knew what he was trying to tell me. I said I was going to fetch my sister and bring her to see him. It was as if a weight had been removed. He relaxed back into his pillow. I asked mum what my sister's name was. It was Elizabeth. I set off to drive the two miles to Westcliff.

The house was on a cliff. I parked on the street outside and I could see through the bay window into the front room as I walked up the path. There was a young boy sat at a piano next to a young man and a girl of a similar age sat nearby watching on. I rang the doorbell and it was answered by a very pretty young woman. I asked to speak to Elizabeth Buffet, my sister's married name, and without asking who I was she said that she was Elizabeth and I was the brother she'd never met. She said that she always knew I would find her one day and that she'd know me straight away. We embraced, both in tears, there on the doorstep. She invited me in for a cup of tea. I could hear piano music coming from the front room. She said it was her son James and her daughter Ella who were having their weekly lesson. We sat and drank tea as she told me about her life and marriage. Her husband John Buffet was a well educated man with a good job in academia. He would be home from work soon. I explained that I was a dance teacher in London and she said that Ella loved dance and had just passed her bronze medal exam at a school in Leigh on Sea. It was in the blood maybe! Then I told her about dad being in hospital and how he had tried to write 'Daughter' then Nan telling me about her and where she lived. It was all so hurried. I'd hardly had time to take it in. Two hours ago I had no idea she existed and now here we were together. I asked if she'd come to see dad. She said of course she would as soon as her husband got in from work. I had been gone too long though and told her I had to get back. She said she'd follow on and I left. I discovered later that she had been in regular contact with our father but hadn't seen him for some time, no doubt as a result of his recent reclusive behaviour. Dad had married Elizabeth's mother, who I never met, in the East End in the 1940's. She was twelve years older than me. It was an incredible experience meeting my sister for the first time like that. I wondered how I'd feel, how she'd feel but you know there was an immediate bond between us. It was as if a long forgotten dream suddenly came true. I could see my father in her eyes.

We sat up with dad until late. Though he wasn't very responsive I'm sure he knew that Elizabeth and I were there and it comforted him. She was very loving. I stayed the night in my old bedroom. It was just as it was when I left right down to the posters on the wall. The house was cold and empty though. It was a house of ghosts. The ghosts of my childhood and of my mother and fathers love. I found a photo album by dad's bed and sat looking through it and drinking whiskey into the early hours. It was his life captured in frozen moments. I don't think I'd ever loved him more. A few hours later the phone rang. It was the hospital telling me my father had died. It was early morning, I drove there to be with him. When I arrived I told a nurse that I'd come to see my father, Alfred Lloyd, and she said that he was 'quite perky' this morning. He was still alive! She led me to a room but it was not dad's room and it was not dad. It was a different man. I collapsed in agonised confusion and the nurse went to a desk and checked some papers with the sister in charge. After a short time the sister approached me and apologised. There were two Alfred Lloyd's on the ward. The other one was already there when dad was admitted and the nurse I'd spoken to had just come on duty and was unaware of the situation. The sister took me to dad's room and there he was pale and still in death. The mix up was a horrible coincidence that sent shivers down my spine but no-one was to blame. I sat by dad's bed and placed his hand in mine. Such was the passing of Alfred Lloyd, my father.

The day of the funeral was very difficult. I was flooded with emotions. How could I survive without my father's friendship and guidance? He had been a rock, always there, always looking out for me. A large number of mourners turned up, my Auntie Gladys, dad's sister with the pub in London, arrived late, accompanied by a group of men in suits and trilby hats, none of whom I recognised. They stood at the back of the church during the service. It was like a scene from The Godfather. Afterwards at the graveside they all tipped their hats in respect and later, when leaving, they all shook my hand. Their hands were like shovels. They were tough men. The last one said 'If you need anything son, just call me.' It was a kind gesture but, as I said, I had no idea who they were. I asked Auntie Gladys and she replied 'I'll tell you later.' She never did.

After the funeral I went back to stay in the house. The rent to the council was £6 a week and as dad had died the tenancy passed to me. I was very lonely and sad. Now the need to drink vodka kicked in. It was not a pleasant social activity any more, it was a dark compulsion. It had become a need, a drug, a friend, a companion I couldn't do without. My mind was out of control. Unbidden thoughts and images rolled and tumbled around inside my brain without respite. Everything was negative and I couldn't see a way forward.

Then out of the blue my Mum told me that she was pregnant by Mr Wonderful, who had turned out to be a notorious breaker up of marriages and a serial deceiver of women. Their short 'romance' ended with Mum abandoned and heart-broken. One good thing came out of this mess however, the birth of another brother Stewart Lloyd! Yes mum decided to give him my Dad's name. She told me that having made a huge mistake in getting involved with Mr Wonderful she wanted to give Stewart the same name as his elder brothers, the name of a Man who had truly loved her. With eyes full of tears she said "I know I've been foolish" then looking down at the baby she was carrying "but I've ended up with something precious". It was very emotional. Mum was hurting a lot, the joy of the new baby dimmed by the memories of deceit and guilt. She rocked gently in her chair. I leant forward, gave her a hug and told her that I loved her. We agreed to draw a line under the past. We all make mistakes and we all regret them but we can't let them define us. We have lives to lead. We have to get on with it.

That said I still had my father's death to deal with and it continued to tear me apart. I felt angry, cheated that I had lost him when I was so young. Why should it be me who had the older dad? What if I hadn't gone to London? What if I'd stayed home, been less selfish? I was embittered, railing against fate. I became irrational. I think I had some sort of mental breakdown. I was travelling between London and Benfleet regularly during this period. I'd stay a couple of nights in the London flat, depending on my teaching agenda and who I was seeing at the time, then go back to Benfleet when I could with various girls in tow. I was living two crazy lives at the same time. During the day, with the distraction of teaching, I felt okay but at night, life became almost unbearable. The same dark thoughts would churn through my mind, the same unanswerable questions. I started having terrible dreams from which I'd wake shaking in horror. My life was spiralling out of control. I didn't realise that the alcohol was making things worse. I thought the opposite in fact. I thought it was helping me. Such is the nature of booze. It wasn't an overnight thing,

I'd been drinking regularly and heavily since I first moved to London. The social scene in the dance world revolved around alcohol and I embraced it without a second thought. It had become a habit and I never saw any danger signs. I wasn't short of money either. At the time I was on TV at least ten times a day dancing in the Marvel Milk advert. Actor Ron Moody, who'd got me the job, lived just a couple of miles from me and acted as my agent, Mr 10%. I received £150 for the initial filming at Shepperton Studios then a repeat fee every time the ad was aired. I'd receive monthly cheques for £1,500, not bad for 1975! I'd buy bottles of spirits from the supermarket in Benfleet with crisp, new notes drawn from the bank. I knew it would be humiliating for Mike Scaratt who'd be sweeping up or stacking shelves to witness this. I'd spend his weekly salary in one visit. I even took Cherry Popwell, wearing a T Shirt with 'I Love to Dance' written on the front, shopping with me on one occasion and deliberately paraded her in front of him. Yes, I was gloating. What an arsehole I had become. Slowly but steadily I came to my senses and felt ashamed of my pettiness. To deliberately belittle another person in front of others is an abominable thing to do even if you have cause to dislike them. It was pathetic. I guess I had reached rock bottom and was just grasping at anything to make me feel better. I thought of my dad's heavy drinking and how I had vowed to myself that I would never gamble or drink like that I didn't like myself or the addiction that I now had and I vowed to defeat it.

Staying in the house in Benfleet soon became unbearable and though I had the opportunity to buy it outright for six thousand pounds I chose not to. I locked the front door, put the key through the letterbox and walked away. When in Essex after that I stayed with my Nan, Uncle Jim and Auntie Rina. Theirs was a domestic normality that was just what I needed at that time. I'd sit in the kitchen and listen to my young cousins Martin and Mandy playing their little games together and my Aunt and Nana gossiping while cooking dinner and all would be right with the world. I even went to Bingo with them one night. The hall was in the British Legion just next door to where they lived so it was no great effort and, much to my surprise, it was quite fun. My Nan's cursing seared the paint off the walls. Bingo is a surprisingly brutal game. I began to smile again. The black cloud started to lift. It was a reminder of the importance of family love and support. There is nothing that matters more. I am sure that without it things would have taken an even darker turn. It's a lesson that has stayed with me to this day. That was a very bad time in my life. It is hard to describe mental illness to someone who has not experienced it. It is a place where nothing is real or as it should be – a dark forest full of shadows. I have never allowed myself to get into such a state again. 1975 was the worst year of my life. But enough of that ….

Chapter 8

'The first time ever I saw your face'

Following that terrible year in my life I was back in London trying to put my troubles behind me. I decided to visit the Top of the Pops studio. This was a place to lift your spirits, exciting and full of fun. It was a hive of activity with an army of production and crew members buzzing around with various pop stars being starry. The atmosphere was very much like the Ballroom Dancing World with everyone competing for the number one slot. My attention was quickly grabbed by the professional dancers who were rehearsing on a surprisingly small stage. I recognised a couple from The Pussycat. One in particular caught my eye. Her name was Paris, she was a great mover and was absolutely gorgeous. I ogled her unashamedly and she smiled back. It was sexual attraction footloose and fancy free, and we both knew it. After the show had finished we left together and went back to my flat where we discussed Einstein's Theory of Relativity until dawn!

I was teaching at The Regency a few days later; it was very busy the buzzer ringing repeatedly as pupils arrived. I opened the studio door for the umpteenth time and found myself face to face with Miss Alyson Bacon, her dance partner and her mother. It was quite a shock, they were the last people I expected to see but I was very pleased. I'd never been able to shake her from my thoughts. We greeted each other and I welcomed them in. She was delightfully cold, a little scornful even, feigning amazement that I'd remembered her name. I told her I would never forget how wonderfully she'd danced at Worcester. She shrugged the compliment off, dismissively commenting that the other judges had scored her just as high that day and I'd never given her a decent mark since. Her mother told her to behave herself. While she sat down to change her shoes I excused myself and went over to the record player to put on 'Can't Take My Eyes Off Of You' by Andy Williams. I smiled over at Alyson but she didn't smile back. She just glared at me fiercely with her razor brown eyes. I pointed her out to Patric, told him that she was the girl I'd raved to him about and asked his opinion. He replied that I was asking the wrong bloke but she seemed alright to him and he intended to tell her mother to keep her locked up away from me. I said it wouldn't be necessary because she'd done nothing but frown at me since they'd arrived. He said she was wise beyond her years. I carried on with my lessons in a distracted fashion. Like the song said I couldn't take my eyes off her. I approached her at the end of the session and asked if she and her mother were staying in London for the weekend. They were. They'd arrived early for a competition on the Sunday. I suggested they come to The Hendon the following evening for my practice class. I promised I'd make them a cup of tea. Mrs Bacon said it sounded a very attractive offer. Alyson said she'd 'think about it.'

I found it hard to sleep that night. I couldn't stop thinking of her. I'd close my eyes and there she'd be. It wasn't just physical attraction either. Don't get me wrong that was definitely part of it but there was something else. She wasn't just beautiful, she was wonderful. I was entranced by her.

The next evening at The Hendon found me in a state of

nervous anticipation, searching through the record collection for the most romantic ones while all the time glancing over at the door to see who was arriving. Anne commented that I was acting strangely and she suspected there was something afoot. I poo poo'd the idea and gave her a playful kiss on the cheek for being so silly. She laughed and called me a very naughty boy. I put 'Under the Moon of Love' on the record player and when I looked up there was Alyson, standing in the open doorway looking just stunning. I smiled broadly and went to greet her. She raised one perfect eyebrow very slightly and gave an imperious 'Hello' in response. This wasn't going to be easy. I introduced her, her mother and her partner to Anne and went to make the promised cup of tea as they took a seat in the rapidly filling ballroom. Sydney came out of the office and Anne told him that I'd been like a kid with a new puppy since the pretty Welsh girl turned up. Sydney had noticed the endless torrent of romantic records I'd been playing and concurred with Anne that this was serious. They left together and I carried on with the evening. The cups of tea, which I nervously spilt into the saucers, were appreciated nonetheless and though I didn't get the smile I'd been hoping for I felt that this was the beginning of something special and indeed it was.

Alyson and her mother came to several more practise classes at the Hendon over the next few weeks and on Saturday 12th of June 1976 Mrs Bacon, with whom I was getting on with very well, invited me to their home in the Mumbles for the following weekend. Alyson was not over enthusiastic but her mum insisted. I said that I was free that weekend, which was an out and out lie, and I'd love to go. Mrs Bacon extolled the beauty of the local beaches and I said I loved beaches which was another lie and we arranged to travel down together on the following Sunday morning. When Alyson started dancing I excused myself, went to the phone booth and cancelled all of my weekend appointments. I wasn't going to miss out on this. At the end of the evening when leaving, Mrs Bacon went to the ladies and I walked Alyson down the stairs to wait for her mother by the glass entrance doors. We could hear the music playing softly from above. Alyson looked up at the black night sky then turned to me and said 'I love the stars.' There was something about that moment, being there with her, I just lost all control, pulled her to me and kissed her on the lips. She pushed me back and asked what I thought I was doing. I smiled and pulled her toward me again but this time she shoved me away angrily and warned me that if I ever did that again! The look on her face made it crystal clear that I could expect a vigorous knee in the nether regions if not worse. I got the message and was about to apologise when we were interrupted by her mother coming down the stairs. She asked what we'd been talking about. 'Just the stars Mrs Bacon' I replied as innocent as a choirboy, 'Just the stars.' We said goodnight and they walked off. There is a piece of received wisdom that if a girl looks back at you when parting she is interested. Alyson looked back but her expression was one of annoyance not interest. She was sending me a reminder of my faux pas in case I'd forget. She was a stern little thing. It was very impressive.

The following week seemed endless. I found myself looking in the studio mirrors more than usual, checking myself out, wondering what the problem was. Maybe I'd lost something, a bit of my famous allure. Maybe I was too thin, a bit more weight might look better. Nothing seemed right. Alyson was on my mind constantly. I lost all interest in other girls. I spoke to Syd about it, told him how I felt. He said I'd be better off without complications in my life and that there were plenty more fish in the ocean but this was one complication I couldn't ignore.

We travelled to Swansea by coach. Alyson was wearing bright yellow Polly Peck trousers with a matching top and she looked gorgeous but it was clear that she still hadn't forgiven me for my previous behaviour and I had to watch my step. We sat together throughout the long journey and chatted, mainly about the dance world. One of Alyson's best friends Lissa James lived near her. Lissa danced with her twin brother Dale, referred to as The Twins. They were dancing stars at the top of their game and had won a bucketful of championships and medals over the years. They were the original Twins from Twin Town, Swansea. The coach trip turned out better than I'd expected. We talked about all kinds of things as well as dance, family, friends, likes, dislikes, I even managed to make her laugh once or twice until that is I got carried away and tried to hold her hand. Her Medusa stare hit me like an electric shock. I let go immediately and we reverted to sitting in cold silence. Then without warning she unleashed a tirade of questions on why I had given her bad marks in the past when judging certain dance championships. I had always given her top marks as a junior then she had a change of partner which didn't work for me and I explained that my marking reflected this. I tried to defend myself by explaining that she had always been my favourite dancer and I was just trying to be scrupulously fair. I was wondering by now if some part of her aggressive attitude had been triggered by my judging and not just my wandering lips, 'First he gives me bad marks and then he has the audacity to expect a kiss!' Looking at it like that you could see her point.

Alyson's father met us at the bus station and drove us to their house in the Mumbles. Philip was a sweet man who became a dear friend. He was a musician by profession, a fellow of The Royal College of Music and a child prodigy having appeared on BBC Radio playing one of

Rachmaninoff's Piano Concerto's when he was just 8 years old.

In the fifties and sixties he'd run the resident dance band at the prestigious Dolphin Hotel in Swansea where they performed with all the great cabaret artists of the era. After the band split up he played the piano for a whole host of name singers before eventually becoming a private teacher. Alyson's Mum, Winifred known as Wyn, had also been in the music business as a singer fronting her own accordion band. She too had been on BBC Radio in company with the likes of Vera Lynn, Dorothy Squires and Pearl Johnson. They were a perfect couple and their love for each other, and their family, was unhidden. The rest of the household was made up of a brother Michael, a very gentle almost timid man 10 years Alyson's senior, Gwyneth, Winifred's sister, who had played a big part in Alyson's upbringing as a regular baby sitter and loving aunt, and her three children Alyson's cousins Susan, Peter and Nest. I had come from a similar eclectic mix and found the domestic environment friendly and welcoming ... thank god!

That summer was the hottest since before the war. We went to the beach at Bracelet Bay the next day. The sun was like a ball of fire and the sky was blue and cloudless. What better way to cool off than a dip in the sea followed by a siesta lying on the soft sand next to the girl of my dreams. I was in paradise then, feeling relaxed and easy, I made my, by now seemingly habitual mistake of complimenting her, telling her how beautiful she looked in her bikini and oops! The shutters came down and she turned her back on me. I just stared at the sky, and thought to myself, well it doesn't matter if the moon and stars are out or sunny blue skies are above us I don't seem to be able to do anything right. I was contemplating my next move when I had an unsettling epiphany. This was a whole new ball game for me, a girl who wasn't easy, didn't giggle at my jokes, wasn't throwing herself at my feet, quite the opposite in fact. I was being rejected. It was the first time I'd ever found myself in this position. I'd always just had to snap my fingers and they'd come running. What was going on? My ego deflated like an old party balloon. I was overwhelmed with uncertainty and doubt. Away from the bright lights of London the great lover was just another boy trying to woo a girl. My depression was standing there in the wings. That was the first time I realised what a selfish bastard I had become. My recent life had been lived almost exclusively in the closed, incestuous bubble of the Dance World. The only time I'd stepped out from it was when I needed to face a real life tragedy and then I would rush back as soon as I could. It was my refuge, a place where self reflection was unnecessary. What had this unnatural isolation done to me? What had I allowed myself to become. Whatever it was I didn't want to be it anymore. I could see what I wanted now and how I had to change to get it. It was a daunting challenge but one I had to take on. The biggest prize of my life lay right next to me on the burning sands of Bracelet Bay. I vowed that I would not let it slip through my fingers.

The following day we found ourselves alone in the house and Alyson decided to cook dinner. An hour or so later she emerged from the kitchen with two plates overflowing with what she called Spaghetti Bolognese. It was pasta with diced corned beef and a tin of tomato soup poured over the top. I said it looked delicious and ate the lot. That was the first of many memorable culinary experiences that I lied about. I mean have you ever had a mushy pea and baked bean sandwich. I don't recommend it. The weekend passed in the blink of an eye but as I was packing to return to London, Wyn came into my room and said that I would be welcome to stay a little longer if I wanted. I didn't need asking twice. I threw my swimming trunks back over the radiator and ended up staying on and off for the next three months, commuting to and from London to teach and Judging all around the country but always returning to the Mumbles. During this time Alyson and I grew closer. Things went slowly at first but a trust was growing. After a time she would walk along the beach holding my hand and an innocent kiss was occasionally allowed. We laughed a lot, I adored her, couldn't be without her. If I wasn't in Wales by her side I was on the phone listening to her sweet voice. When you are falling in love with someone everything about them is perfect isn't it and I was certainly falling in love.

We celebrated Alyson's seventeenth birthday on the 11th of October with a party at the house but I had to leave at an unearthly hour the next morning to get the first train back to London. She filled my thoughts throughout the day and when I called that night I asked her to marry me. She was taken aback and didn't actually answer. I told her to take her time and think about it. The following weekend I booked a table at The Stoneleigh Club in Porthcawl and took the family out for a slap up dinner. I'd booked the centre table right in front of the stage and when we arrived I got the waiter to bring us two bottles of champagne with a dozen glasses and I constructed a champagne tower on the table. This mysterious behaviour was only explained when I began pouring the fizzy stuff into the top glass and, to everyone's delight it cascaded down in a fountain. I handed out the filled glasses and we toasted Mr and Mrs Bacon's marriage.

I had two glasses all evening, a far cry from the Champagne Charlie of just several months ago. Phil asked me where I'd learned the trick with the glasses and was highly impressed when I told him I'd seen George Best doing it in a London nightclub. The lights went down and the cabaret was introduced. It was the international singing star Peter Gordeno who opened with 'Fever'. He was excellent and his two accompanying dancers were top notch too. His second number was dedicated to 'Miss Alyson Bacon' who he sought out in the audience and kissed on the hand before doing 'Put a Little Love in your Heart' right up close and sexy. Alyson was suitably embarrassed but her mum and dad loved it. It was well worth the fifty quid. When they left the table to dance I asked Alison if she'd considered my offer of marriage further. She said she had … and she was looking upon it favourably. A few weeks later I arranged a weekend in Lowestoft for Alyson, her Mum and Auntie Nin. On the Saturday night we went to a club called The Talk of the East, I did the champagne glass trick again then got down on one knee and proposed with a diamond ring instead of a telephone call. She said yes.

I was judging a competition in Exeter, for Frank and Jackie Tagg soon after and Alyson came along with me. Her mum wasn't entirely happy with us going off alone and only agreed when I assured her I'd drive Alyson back the same night, a foolish but expedient promise I was desperate to find a way of breaking. Well, it seemed that the gods of love were smiling down on me because a blizzard arrived on the afternoon of the competition and the roads became thick with snow. The forecast said it was in for the next few days. Alyson phoned her mum and, with an element of hyperbole, convinced her that we'd become snowed in and had no choice but to stay where we were until it cleared. At the end of the day we went back to the nearby hotel where I had been booked in and … well, we had to do something to keep warm … right.

The above description of that night is flippant and horribly inadequate. This is because even now all these years later I find it desperately hard to do justice to the wonder of it. To be there in that hotel room, with the snow falling outside, in the company of the girl I loved, the girl who had agreed to become my wife, to lay with her for the first time, to touch her perfect skin, to hold her in my arms, to kiss her …. Many had loved before us I know but that night in that hotel room was ours and ours alone. Imagine a bird born and raised in a cage one day being freed.

One night Alyson told me that she was adopted. She was very emotional and it was obviously something that meant a lot to her. When she was just six weeks old Phil and Wyn, her new Mum and Dad, picked her up from the children's home in Cwmdonkin, Swansea. She wasn't aware of this until years later another eight year old girl mocked her by saying 'You haven't got a real mum and dad, you're adopted.' in front of the other children in the school play-ground. When she got home she asked Phil and Wyn what the girl had meant and they told her the truth. They said they always intended to tell her when she was older and they were proved right to have decided to leave it until later by the very fact of it being so upsetting and confusing for her when she did find out at that tender age. When she told me this story in her own words and with her obvious emotion, I just hugged her and cried. She already knew about my strange origins and I told her that it was just another of the many things that linked us together in such a perfect way. The dear girl had got over it by now and could not have loved her mum and dad more but these things, these shreds from the past can linger all one's life. She had me now to take care of her and I had her. We had each other. In the spring of 1977 Alyson moved into my flat in Earls Court with me. My mum had always wanted a daughter but had three boys. When I introduced her to Alyson she loved her as much as I did. They became best friends. It wasn't long before we were in a financial position to buy mum a new washing machine, tumble dryer, cooker and some good furniture. It was wonderful to see mum so comfortable and Alyson made sure she wanted for nothing, another reason why my girl is so special.

This was a very happy time with Alyson in my life, my private lessons book full and judging jobs still pouring in though I couldn't help but be curious as to why I was in such demand as a judge. Maybe it was due to the fact that I wouldn't be swayed or corrupted, I marked on talent alone. The couples I marked to win were often total strangers to me but in my judgement they were the best. This meant that my own pupils would often have to take lower marks from me of course which obviously didn't please them but they understood that that was the way it was. The thing is I know firsthand the amount of hard work and dedication that is required to become the best on floor and to have some self righteous, crooked judge mark their own undeserving couples first is a crime against the profession. Unfortunately whether it's Ice Skating, Gymnastics or even Boxing wherever you have judges you have the opportunity for corruption. Obviously you need to be quick when judging Ballroom as the music only lasts a few minutes per dance. I had my own method, an initial scan of the floor for a quick look at each couples overall position of the hold, body frame, footwork, technique and timing, in Latin American the rhythm, hip action, musicality, technique and then the different characteristics of the specific dances. Each blink of the eye was like taking a photograph and saving it in my brain along with an initial Poor, Average or Good assessment then a second scan marking down the numbers and a third to make sure. My adrenaline would be flowing, the music, the dancing, the atmosphere, the pressure would all play a part and the responsibility for getting it right was always on my mind. To sum it up it's like going to the theatre to watch your favourite show and getting paid handsomely for doing it. However, as I say, some judges tackled it in a different way, scanning the floor to find the numbers of their own couples first. I recall standing next to a very high profile adjudicator who wrote the numbers of his two couples on his judging pad before the music had even started. I also came across judges who would consistently mark the best couples last until they were forced to give in and have lessons with them to win over their support. Having lessons with particular judges to gain their votes is a fairly common occurrence which can occasionally get you more than you bargained for. I had a lesson once with a Latin specialist who was more interested in the sexual allure of my partner than teaching us anything. It was like having a Rumba lesson with a randy octopus, his hands were everywhere. We never returned. Holding couples to ransom by using your position for your personal gain and gratification is quite despicable. It was sad to see that someone I had looked up to as a boy could behave in that way.

I've lost count of the times that I witnessed the disappointment when dancers were cheated out of their rightful rewards. Knowing and experiencing this first hand was in fact the main reason I didn't want to be a competitive dancer. I have great admiration for those who do and ride out the storm to enjoy success and the camaraderie and respect of the majority of professionals and judges who operate honestly and fairly within the dance world. That takes determination, self belief and guts.

Today we have 'The Curse of Strictly', a tabloid term for when a celebrity contestant gets involved romantically with their professional dance partner on the highly successful BBC TV show 'Strictly Come Dancing'. It is often front page news but I assure you it is nothing new, the dance world has been 'at it' for years. In fact 'Strictly...' is nowhere near as racy as the real thing. I know dancers who have to stop and think for a while before answering the question 'How many times have you been married?' or 'How many affairs have you had since you've been married?' It's a simple formula, romantic music, close physical contact, the drama, two bodies becoming one on the dance floor, take your eye off the ball for a moment and whoops! Some would say in the words of the great George Gershwin 'Nice work if you can get it'! The negative side of course is the pain of betrayal, broken marriages and a sometimes character deforming cynicism. A price worth paying? Not for me.

Chapter 9

'Staying Alive'

Sydney was worried. The Hendon wasn't getting the numbers it had been and paying the rent was becoming a problem. It was the same for schools all over the country. The world was moving on and it seemed that learning to dance wasn't high on people's lists of priorities. Some schools were closing down. It was a disturbing trend. I was worried too. This was my chosen profession and I could see it slipping away. The problem as far I could see was that we hadn't adjusted to keep up with the changes in society. We offered the same thing as we'd offered for the last fifty years. It was a wonderful thing of course but to many, particularly the young, it was a remnant of a bygone age. The only nod to modernity had been the inclusion of The Jive in the early sixties as an acknowledgement of Rock and Roll and by 1977 even that was old hat. The new music was punk rock and the new dance was hopping up and down on the spot and pretending to head butt each other and no-one needed professional training to do that. I was still getting teaching and judging work and the situation hadn't affected me directly as yet but it was clear that if things kept going in the direction they were going it wouldn't be long before it did. It wasn't just me either, I had Alyson now. I wasn't just a young hothead living for the moment. I wanted us to have a career together in the job that we'd dedicated so much of our lives to, the job we loved. I have never been a religious man, even as a child I hadn't bought into it, but that doesn't mean that I don't believe in anything. I toyed with the idea that life isn't just a random sequence of events and that of course infers that there might be some extra physical source of order. I don't presume to know its nature but there are times, when a lonely man finds love, when the despairing find hope, when a seemingly insoluble problem is solved by chance for instance when, for want of a better word, 'fate' seems to intervene. This was one of these times and it was to send Alyson and my careers soaring and equally, if not more, importantly rescue the world of Dance Teaching from what seemed to be its imminent and certain decline.

The Hendon was situated above a cinema as The Western had been. This made sense as the upper levels of such buildings have the same large floor area as the picture house below which makes them perfect for dance studios. I'd go to watch films from time to time, often in the afternoons in the break between morning and evening lessons. I was still dealing with my depression and it helped take my mind off things. I attended an afternoon matinee of a new film one Saturday and was surprised to find the place packed to the rafters with people my own age and younger. Not only that but there was a queue outside a few hundred yards long that couldn't get in but were waiting for the next showing. I only got in because I knew the box office people. I settled down with my ice cream and chocolate and prepared to be entertained. After twenty minutes or so I was totally involved in what was going on, on screen. The film was fresh, it was different. The actors didn't seem like actors, they seemed like people I knew and it wasn't just me either, the whole audience was rapt. We laughed at the jokes, we listened in silence to the drama, we empathised with the plight of the young people being shown. It was an incredible experience and the most incredible thing about it was that it had the most fabulous dancing at its core. The dance and the music were so perfect, so of the time that watching the film became an almost mystical experience for everyone there. When it ended the place erupted in an applause that lasted a full five minutes. There was a buzz as we left the cinema. People were embracing, telling those in the queue what a treat they had in store. There was a mood of communal joy and affection that I had never felt before. We had shared something special and I couldn't wait to tell Sydney.

I bounded up the stairs to The Hendon and told him that I had found the solution to the dance teaching world's problem. The machinery of the universe had dictated that I turn up at that very cinema on the very afternoon 'Saturday Night Fever' was playing and had shown me the answer. The film was sexy, funny, dramatic and thrilling. I implored Sydney to give disco lessons a try. He said it sounded like shit and I was wasting my time. I pleaded with him to at least go down to the next showing and see for himself and he eventually gave way. When he got back he said he was now sure that it was shit, a passing fad. He'd fallen asleep half way through. I asked him to give my idea one shot, to put an advertisement in The Hendon Times along the lines of 'YOU'VE SEEN THE FILM, YOU'VE HEARD THE MUSIC, NOW LEARN THE DANCE!' I told him he had nothing to lose. I even offered to pay for the ad out of my own pocket. Reluctantly, to please me, he agreed. 'One advert and that's it!' I spent the next week listening to the soundtrack album, watching the film four more times, and making notes of the dance moves by the light of the flickering screen. Alyson and I worked on the routines together day and night. We made up five line dances from the notes. On the day the ad was published in The Hendon Times a huge queue appeared outside the studio. Sydney looked out of the window and assumed it was for the picture house but it wasn't. It was a second queue, an equally large and equally excited queue waiting for us to open our doors. They wanted to learn how to boogie. I put 'Stayin'Alive' on the record player to greet them as they poured in. Sydney had to help Anne at the door, she was overwhelmed, and there were still hundreds waiting in the queue outside. If anything the more people we let in the longer the queue seemed to get. Sydney stopped admitting them at one point saying there were so many I'd have no room to teach them but I told him that that since it was line dancing we could get them all facing the same way and If he'd operate the music from the stage I'd stand on the tea bar counter to teach. I said he should pack them in which he did. The place was heaving and there was still an enormous queue waiting outside. Anne asked what we could do with them and I told her to tell them to wait and I'd do another class after this one had finished. She did and they did. Sydney stood by the record player surveying the scene and grinning like a Cheshire cat. I could see the sparkle of filthy lucre in his eyes.

I climbed onto the tea bar counter and faced the crowd. I was wearing a pair of 28 inch, high waisted, dusky pink flared trousers, and a pink and white shirt. I shouted out 'Are you ready for Night Fever?' And they screamed a passionate 'Yes' in reply. I demonstrated the first moves several times then gave Sydney the nod to put the track on. I counted them in and everyone began to move to the music. The mood was ecstatic. The crowd outside could hear the music and were itching to get in, to be a part of it. At the end of the lesson Sydney announced that the next lesson would be the following night at the same time. There was a huge cheer and the pupils left buzzing with enthusiasm and chattering with delight. Sydney was the happiest I'd ever seen him. He was stunned that it had been such a huge success. The next lot were let in and were just as involved and happy as the first, even more so if anything. After they'd left Sydney opened the drinks cabinet and we shared a cigar and a beer to celebrate.

This was the start of it all. The Fever was catching! Over the next few weeks we packed them in every night. I was the only person who wasn't surprised. I was already familiar with disco from my social life and knew that it was fun and socially inclusive. I'd been in clubs where the fever had taken hold. I knew it firsthand. Why it took the film to spark the idea I don't know. I should have thought of it anyway but that said I am eternally grateful to John Travolta et al for their wonderful creation. It made me realise that it was no good just selling a dance, it was necessary to sell the lifestyle the dance represented. Ballroom had come to represent a faded past, a world of dinner suits and gowns, of shiny wooden floors lit by glitter balls, a world of middle class aspiration. It was old fashioned. It was boring. Disco, the disco of Club 54 and 'Saturday Night Fever' was new and wild and exciting. It sold working class sex. It was a drug. People just couldn't get enough of it.

It wasn't long before Patric wanted us to take some classes in Wimbledon. He'd also arranged his own teacher's workshops and booked me to run them. He billed it as 'Disco Workshops by George Lloyd Himself!' Miss Haylor called me shortly after and invited me over to arrange some Disco classes at The Mardi. Marion Brown was going to take the classes so I spent half a day preparing her with the line dances. One of the classes she taught was made up of a group of young well bred young ladies including Lady Diana Spencer. She was only seventeen at the time and hadn't yet entered the public consciousness as she was destined to do. In fact she was quite shy but nonetheless had a glowing presence about her. Her parents had obviously chosen The Mardi for their daughter to attend because of the connection between them and Phyllis's partner Nerina who was the author of a book about the Spencer family.

Alyson gave up competition dancing to work with me and though it was inevitable it was also a shame because she had already enjoyed significant success as a competitor. She had a unique style and an abundance of natural talent and it was thought by many that with the right partner she could have got to the top. I felt guilty about this decision at the time but we both agreed it was the right thing to do. Alyson soon mastered the technique and was very successful in her teacher's exams and this together with the creative flair she had for choreography made her a great teacher and a perfect partner for me to work with when creating new routines. She was my inspiration.

The film 'Grease' came out shortly after 'Saturday Night Fever' and I was back in the cinema with my little notepad once again hungrily devouring the moves. As with Fever the music was great and we soon garnered another batch of line dances to keep up with demand. John Travolta felt like a long lost brother. I'm afraid that I became a bit of a clone, the swagger, the hair combing, the smile but who could blame me. Was he not the coolest thing since Elvis! At least I didn't speak in an American accent … not often anyhow. Sydney didn't need any persuasion this time. As soon as I mentioned the film he just said without hesitation 'What do you want me to put in the advert?' Dance teachers from all over the UK came to us hungry for our knowledge. Their schools which, like The Hendon, had been on their knees soon became busier than ever. There is no doubt that this new form of dance saved many dance schools from closure during the 1970's. This was just the beginning. Things were moving fast, like 'Greased Lightening'.

Someone threw a pebble at the window of my flat early one morning. It was Sydney. He wanted to see me then and there. It was something very important. After a quick shower I shot around to the studio. He'd had had a call from the Imperial Society. They wanted me to give a lecture to the annual congress at Cecil Sharpe House. I was dumbstruck. This was an enormous honour. I went to see Miss Haylor at The Mardi. She'd already heard the news. I told her I was delighted but also quite nervous. She was her usual wonderful, phlegmatic, kind self and after showing her some of my planned material she assured me I had nothing to worry about. She reminded me that I had the element of surprise on my side. I could take it where I wished. As for being nervous I was to imagine the audience of my betters and peers all sat on toilet seats, a setting where no man or woman can lord or lady it over any other. I loved the idea. I took Miss Haylor out to tea to thank her for her friendship and advice. This time I was fully prepared for the little sandwiches and cakes that came along with it. Her efforts had not gone entirely to waste. I was becoming sophisticated.

The big day arrived. Alyson and I were in the changing room at Cecil Sharpe House preparing ourselves for action. Outside, waiting for us in the adjoining ballroom, was an audience of all the Imperial Society's professional dance teachers with the cream, Bill and Bobbie Irvine, Peter Eggleton, Miss Haylor, Peter Pearson and others sat together at the top table. I was wearing a pair of black 28inch waisted trousers with a red open neck shirt and Alyson was in a red dress. I was bricking it. In fact I thought I was going to vomit. I only hoped I'd do it before going on stage. My made to measure trousers were bloody tight too. I think my voice went up a register or two. We could hear the expectant hum of the crowd. Then we were announced, the lights dimmed and 'Stayin' Alive' burst out over the PA system. I appeared from the shadows and started strutting around the floor swinging a tin of paint, which is what Travolta's character Tony Manero does at the top of the film. The audience were delighted and started clapping along to the music and cheering me on. I spotted Bob and Marion Barber, my first teachers, at the far end of the ballroom looking delighted and that filled me with warmth. As I turned to head back up towards the top table my nerves disappeared and I was possessed of a beautiful calm excitement. The music just carried me along. When I reached the top table I swung the lidless tin of paint and released the confetti it contained all over the big wigs sitting there. The audience burst into laughter. I put the tin down and the music ended. I walked to the centre of the room and introduced myself and my partner Alyson Bacon. Alyson was not there! I looked around and finally down to see that she had slipped on the confetti and had slid underneath the piano. Bobbie Irvine was helping her up, both of them laughing their socks off. The audience soon joined in. I don't know to this day whether they thought it was a part of the routine or not but who cares. When you're hot you can get away with anything. Alyson joined me and we started by giving a demonstration of the line dance to 'Night Fever.' We gave it the full treatment and it ended to an explosion of applause. The atmosphere was crackling. Then we invited those who wished to, to join us on the floor to learn the dance. There was a huge rush. It seemed that everyone wanted to be in on it. We finished our lecture with a demonstration to 'More Than a Woman.' By Tavares and the place went wild. There was a prolonged standing ovation and we were patted on the back and congratulated by everyone as we made our way back to the dressing room. Afterwards Bob and Marian invited us back to The Western to teach for a day. We were both so elated. We flew without wings. It didn't get much better than this.

Our day teaching at The Western was a joy though it was undeniably strange being back where I started, teaching my own first teachers. They made it easy though with their kindness and grace. They were much more than my teachers by now. They were dear friends. Impressed by our lecture at Cecil Sharpe the Imperial Society asked me to write a book on disco dancing with a view to using it as a syllabus for examinations. Not knowing what I was letting myself in for I said yes. It was a mammoth task. I could never have done it without Alyson who worked on it tirelessly and diligently with me in our new house in Hampshire. We were awake working into the early hours every night. Our dear friend Grace Hunt was awake with us making notes and typing them up as Alyson and I went through the moves. It was much, much harder than dancing. These professional writers really earn their money.

Though hard at it writing the book we still had to fit in our teaching and demonstration work. We were pretty much in constant demand doing shows here, there and everywhere and the diary was full with private lessons. We had become very popular and the shows were spectacularly successful. They had amazing write ups in the trade papers and Alyson and I were heralded as 'Stars'. We even got fan mail. Girls would call out to me in the streets 'Hey Tony are you as good in bed as you are on the dance floor?' a quote from the film, and Alyson got an equal amount of attention from the boys. Lucky our attention was strictly on each other. At the same time as all this we were pursuing our own ventures. We promoted the very first Disco competitions in Camberley, Surrey and back at The Paddocks on Canvey Island. Dance News editor and promoter Bobby Short took an interest and asked me to join him to promote the first Disco Championship at The Cat's Whiskers in Streatham. I agreed to do so and booked Sue Menhenick from Legs And Co. to judge the event which I compared under the watchful eyes of Bobby, his wife Linda and John and Arlene Leach who were viewing and monitoring from the balcony. Half way through Bobby ran down the stairs ready to strangle the DJ who thought it appropriate to offer a free T-shirt to the first lucky girl who would be prepared to put it on there and then. Bobby let him know that this was a serious dance competition not a strip club and the idiot was suitably chastised. Bobby ordered me to keep an eye on him nonetheless. Bobby was a well liked and respected man and I was very proud when he asked me to write a weekly Disco page in the Dance News. I wasn't very good at writing articles which he soon discovered but he kept the page in because it was popular with younger readers. It helped spread the word. The gospel according to Tony Manero was the new religion and George Lloyd was its high priest.

Chapter 10

'How Deep Is Your Love'

Sydney was on the phone to dance teachers all over the country day in and day out raving to them about the new craze that could save their schools. They kept booking in to have private lessons in response and my packed schedule became even more packed. Sydney's close friend, renowned teacher of Latin American World Champions, Nina Hunt was booked in to have disco lessons with me. She was fantastic needless to say. We laughed through the two hours and had a ball. Nina said she was getting requests from overseas teachers to learn the disco moves. The Fever was spreading fast. I am very proud to say that following that lesson many of the teachers who came to me for lessons were sent by the legendary Nina Hunt. Peggy Spencer had arranged for Anne Lingard to come to the Hendon and have private lessons with the aim of learning my routines to teach at Peggy's school. When Peggy realised how much material I had produced and how incredibly popular this new craze had become she phoned Sydney and told him that she intended to form a teachers' workshop. She had already signed up Patricia Thompson, Michael Stylianos and Anne Lingard and she asked Sydney if yours truly would like to join them. I was right up for it. We travelled around the country starting at the Hammersmith Palais, which was sold out with eager teachers from all over the UK packed in, then on to other large venues in Liverpool, Birmingham, and Scotland. The camaraderie with Patricia Michael and Anne made the whole experience very enjoyable. They were all true professionals and with Peggy at the helm presenting her workshops I accepted my position at the bottom of the pecking order without complaint. My position as High Priest had been usurped by Peggy the Abbess!

One afternoon Anne Lingard called in to see me at The Hendon beaming with delight. She told me that I had to put on my swankiest dinner suit and join her at the 1978 Carl Allen Award Ceremony at Grosvenor House, Park Lane the following week. I had been nominated! The news knocked me off my feet. You don't get bigger than this in the British Dance world. This on top of the lecture at Cecil Sharpe, it was dreamlike. I was incredibly proud and excited. I was dancing on air. Five days later my beautiful wife and I found ourselves sat at the bar in the hallowed Great Room of the Grosvenor spruced up and smelling sweet. All the great and the good of the Imperial Society of The Teachers of Dancing were there and I was getting thumbs ups and smiles all round. I was sure that Bill Irvine had a lot to do with my nomination. I thanked him but he brushed it aside. He said that I deserved it and it was nothing to do with him. He advised me to just relax and enjoy the occasion which I eventually started to do. There was a lovely atmosphere in the room with lots of laughter ringing around the tables. As the time approached for the ceremony to begin an anxious looking Anne Lingard pushed her way through the crowd and approached me at the bar. She wanted a word in private. The poor woman had the unenviable task of informing me that Peggy Spencer was to receive the award. Peggy wanted her to tell me before the presentation. It was thoughtful of her and, as I said to Anne, at least it gave me time to prepare a smile. I thanked her for letting me know and kissed her on the cheek. The ceremony passed with an inevitable sense of deflation. People were very kind afterwards, coming up and offering commiserations. Bill Irvine put his hand on my shoulder and said 'You were my winner young man. Better luck next time.' It was a blow and I was down for a few days then I put it behind me. It had however helped kindle a mood of discontent with the dance business that had been smouldering inside me for some time. As we were leaving Grosvenor House, Alyson and I were approached by Huibert Alkema, a dance teacher from Holland with a very healthy bank balance, who invited us to dinner at the Hilton. He was extremely charming especially to Alyson. We accepted and joined him in the rooftop restaurant of the hotel the following evening. He told us that he'd been very impressed by our lecture at the Imperial Society. He came to London often and always made sure to attend such events. He offered Alyson a cigarette which he lit with a very unusual and impressive gold lighter. It doubled up as a pocket calculator, something relatively common now but unheard of in those days. Alyson commented on it and he immediately offered it to her as a gift which she accepted with protests. Then he made us a job offer. He wanted us to go to Holland, to teach in his studio with a house in the country, a brand new car and an extremely generous salary. We thanked him but explained that there were one or two impediments to our accepting, we had to finish the book for one and we were booked up with classes and demonstrations for the rest of the season, we couldn't just renege on our obligations, and we had recently fixed the date of our wedding. He said that none of it was problematic; we could satisfy these commitments and then take up his offer in the autumn when the new season began. Alyson was attracted by there being animals, chickens, ducks and goats with the country house. We both love animals. We could have fresh eggs every day. I asked if there were pigs and he said there would be by the time we got there. Finally he upped his salary offer by twenty five percent. He was a very charming and persuasive man. We shook on it.

After endless days and nights of toil the book was finally finished and Miss Haylor offered us the use of The Mardi for the accompanying photographs. She read through the manuscript and pronounced herself well pleased. It was not exactly War and Peace and I was certainly no Tolstoy but, that said, I was quite proud of it. It covered what it needed to cover and was simple to follow. I offered to take Miss Haylor through some of the routines but she declined. A wise move, it would have been like the Queen twerking! While there I took the opportunity to tell her of our decision to move to Holland. She said that I should do what I thought was right and blessed my decision whatever it was. I told her that I would never forget what she had done for me and that she was the one person I always knew I could trust. She brushed aside my emotional compliment but I could see that she too was touched. I kissed her on the cheek and no more was said. She took her handkerchief from her bag, stood up and walked elegantly from the ballroom. The photographer David Bland arrived and set up shortly after and the rest of the day passed smoothly.

I told Sydney about our planned move shortly after. It wasn't the best news he'd ever had and he made his disappointment clear but my mind was made up. The book had been proof read and was at the printers and Sydney suggested we arrange a Disco Teach In at The Hendon as a launch. I told him that Patric had already booked me for a launch at The Regency. Sydney was even less pleased but we booked a second launch at The Hendon as well to keep the peace. Rivalry had reared its nasty head again. This as much as anything was what I wanted to get away from. I didn't want to be put in these positions where I had to pick sides between friends. Both launches went really well. Patric was sparkling at Wimbledon and the place was abuzz from the word go. Sydney was annoyed because The Hendon's association with my name had attracted a lot of work and he saw that slipping away. There was nothing I could do about that unfortunately. I had my life to lead.

The book was finally published in 1979 not long after the best day of my life. On the 20th of January of that year Alyson Bacon married George Lloyd at The Tabernacle Church, Newton Rd, Mumbles, Swansea, Wales. It was a lavish event with a large number of guests. My best man was my dear mate and fellow dance teacher Rodney Weeks. I didn't have a stag night but Rodney and I got suitably blubbery together the night before in the guest house we were staying at and if it had not been for him it is highly likely I would have missed the most important date I ever had. The reception was held at The Caswell Bay Hotel on the sea front. It was a fiesta of food, drink and dance. Alyson and I did a passionate Rumba to kick things off and the place rocked and swayed till the early hours. It was perfect. I only wished my dad had been there. He would have been so proud. We spent the night at The Dolphin Hotel and the next morning I surprised Mrs Lloyd with the news that I'd booked a honeymoon in Spain. Unfortunately the car decided to overheat on the motorway about fifteen minutes from Luton Airport and I had to walk about half a mile to an emergency telephone to call the breakdown service. It became apparent that we were going to miss our flight. I telephoned the tour operator and explained the situation. They were very sympathetic and said we should get to the check in desk as soon as we could. We got there twenty minutes after the scheduled take off time and the check in was closed. The staff let us through nonetheless and told us to run to the boarding gate with our suitcases. When we got there we were rushed up the steps onto the plane where we were greeted with a loud cheer and round of applause from the other passengers and the crew. The doors were closed immediately and the plane took off a half an hour late. The captain had informed the people on board about the honeymoon couple's plight and asked if they would be prepared to wait. Fortunately for us they all replied in the affirmative. After our seatbelts were discarded the stewardess played the 'Grease' album on a ghetto blaster and we got all our fellow passengers to do the hand jive five thousand feet above the English Channel. It was quite a sight! Mr and Mrs Lloyd went on to share ten days of sun drenched bliss. The good things that had been happening to me were doing the trick as far as combating my depression was concerned. I was feeling like a new man. The old me seemed distant and obsolete. The winter of my discontent was made glorious summer.

A short while after we returned from our honeymoon, Patric came to stay in our Hampshire retreat for a break from the studio. We woke one morning to find that he'd been up early and filled the lounge with flowers from the forsythia bushes in the garden and when I say 'filled' I mean filled. It smelled beautiful but there was hardly anywhere left to sit down. He wasn't one to do things by half. Then he served us a champagne breakfast. We got hazy in the sunlit lounge and talked and laughed like the old friends we had become. We had a very enjoyable few days together. There was never a dull moment with the Duchess around.

Alyson and I appeared on Southern Television's 'Day by Day' to talk about the book. The show began with us doing a dance in which I lifted Alyson high above my head only to be interrupted by Sarah Kennedy, the presenter, saying 'Put her down George!' Following the interview I danced with Sarah and lifted her up. It was a delightfully light note to end on and we got excellent feedback all round. It was great publicity. The book was selling well and the days passed in a blur of lessons and promotional work. The date of our move to Holland arrived in the blink of an eye. We said our farewells, many of them tearful, and left Britain with our entire lives packed into four suitcases. Huibert Alkema met us at Schipol Airport and chauffeured us to the dance studio in the city in his spectacular Mercedes. We chatted on the way and he told us that the arrival of 'The English Stars' was a big thing in Holland. News of our coming had been in all the papers and there was great excitement. People couldn't wait to start learning the new disco moves that were such the rage in Britain. He was looking at Alyson in the rear view mirror a bit too much for my liking but I let it pass. There were crowds of youngsters waiting in the street outside the studio, cheering and shouting out greetings, when we pulled up. Newspaper reporters with cameras took our pictures and yelled out questions as we walked to the entrance. It was like the Oscars. I smiled at Alyson. We were sure then that we had made the right decision. We couldn't have been happier.

The Ballroom was very spacious with a long bar down one side. We sat and had a drink and a look through the various newspapers spread on the counter, most of which had photos of us with matching headlines, 'English Dance Couple coming to Holland.' I noticed that we were named as George Lloyd and Alyson Bacon and pointed out to Huibert that we were in fact both Lloyds having been married for some time. He dismissed it as unimportant and said that the Dutch boys would love the name Alyson Bacon. I tried to put it to the back of my mind but his remarks and his manner made me oddly uncomfortable.

We were very happy living in the big country house with all the animals, the chickens, ducks, goats, sheep and of course pigs. I guess I was a country boy at heart. We only gave classes in the evenings so all the days were free for us to wander and talk and take in the beauty of our surroundings. The lessons themselves were packed every one of them. We made a lot of good friends and learned to speak a faltering Dutch. That summer we threw a big party at the house for all of our new acquaintances. A whole load turned up including most of our dance couples and the day went with a swing. There was lots of bilingual fun around the house and in the grounds. Most of the guests stayed the night and the following morning I had to step over bodies right left and centre as I went to collect the chicken's eggs. The morning was Hangover City as people tried to piece together the hazy events of the previous day. This was Holland after all! Then the phone rang. It was my mum calling to let me know that my dear friend Patric Plumb had died suddenly from a heart attack. He had managed to phone for an ambulance but by the time the paramedics arrived it was too late. I was crushed by this news and retired to my bedroom to be alone. I thought of the last time we met when I said my goodbyes before leaving for Holland. Patric's last words to me were 'Good luck teaching them Dutchies to dance in those bloody wooden clogs.' Even at such a sad time he managed to bring a smile to my face. I remembered the room full of forsythia and thought how he would have enjoyed our party and the famous Dutch gin. He would have held court in the sunshine to a whole new audience. I intended buying him a pair of clogs for Christmas with 'The Duchess' carved into them. He would have loved that.

Terrible things can happen in life, when ill fortune visits without warning, when something wicked crashes into your world uninvited and everything comes tumbling down.

Such a thing was to happen to us. A few weeks after the party I was in the back garden cutting grass when I heard a scream from inside the house. As I ran inside Huibert Alkema, who had been visiting, dashed past me to his car and sped away. Alyson was in the kitchen shaking and in tears. She said that Alkema had tried to kiss her and she'd had to physically fight him off. I wanted to go after him, to confront him, but Alyson said no, that nothing had actually happened and it was better to forget about it. This was on a Sunday, our day off. Despite what Alyson said I decided to go into the dance school that evening when the studio was open for drinks and have it out with him. When I got there he was sitting at the bar. I walked up to him and asked him what he thought he was up to. He just sat there smiling and acted as if he didn't know what I was talking about so I spelt it out to him. He flatly denied anything had happened and just kept smiling at me as if I was a simpleton. I had to control myself. I went to one of the tables and had a beer with Ruurd, one of the dance boys to cool off. I could see Alkema glancing at me occasionally while chatting to a group of young girls, buying them drinks, laughing and playing the big man. I was seething inside. One of my students, a girl about seventeen, came up to speak to me. She asked me where Alyson was and told me that she loved our classes then she asked if I'd like to go to a disco club nearby with her for a drink. I declined the offer but she left it open in case I 'changed my mind' then walked off and joined Alkema's group. I finished my drink and left the studio calling in the gents on the way. When I got outside the same girl, now wearing a very expensive looking fur coat, was draped over the bonnet of my car. She said she hoped I'd changed my mind because she was hot for me and wanted us to drive somewhere and have sex. I told her to get off my bonnet, got in the car and drove home. When I got there

I found Alyson distraught. Alkema had been on the phone trying to talk her around and when she made it clear she wasn't interested the conversation took a sinister turn. He'd told her that I had left the studio earlier with a girl and gone off to have sex with her. Although Alyson didn't believe his lies she still found it upsetting. I explained what had actually happened and we held each other close. What in god's name was Alkema playing at. This was a nasty situation and it was going to get worse.

The next day Alkema phoned to say that our services would no longer be required and we should make our way back to the UK. I contacted the solicitor who drew up the contract and he told me to stay where I was. The contract was binding. A lengthy court battle followed. We appeared in front of the judge with our solicitor who translated everything to us as the case proceeded. Alkema took the witness stand and claimed that I had broken our contract by having sex with one of the students. Next, I must say to my disbelief, the girl in question, still in the fur coat, arrived in person to confirm his story. She glanced repeatedly at Alkema throughout her 'evidence' during which he smiled and nodded encouragement. The girl said that I had driven her to a quiet location where I'd undressed her and we had intercourse. It wasn't a complicated lie and virtually impossible to disprove. Alkema was grinning and flicking imaginary ash off the sleeve of his Armani suit, sensing victory in his vindictive little subterfuge. It seemed that all was lost. Then a miracle happened. Alkema's accountant, Hank Walters, was called to give evidence and, as our solicitor translated, he told the court that Alkema, who he knew well, was a serial adulterer and that his wife had suffered from his mental cruelty for many years. He said that he was convinced that the girl in the fur coat was acting under Alkema's instructions in return for money and other favours and that the entire thing was a set up. He said he felt obliged to speak up out of common decency. He couldn't stand aside and see us being cheated and defamed in this way. He said he found it disgusting. Most vitally he said that he had overheard Alkema's phone call to Alyson, a phone call that he had denied ever making under oath, which of course meant that he could well be lying about everything else. His case was in tatters. At that point Alkema stood up and walked out of the room. The girl followed moments later. The Judge thanked Walters for his candour then turned to Alyson and me and said that our salary would be paid in full for the duration of the contract. He added that he sincerely hoped that this incident wouldn't spoil our opinion of Dutch people in general of which Alkema was a very poor example. There was no danger of that, we'd already met some lovely people and made some good friends there. The Judge wished us both well and a happy life there in Holland. Then he dismissed the case. Alkema was a manipulative narcissist, a despicable man who believed that his position and wealth entitled him to have anything, or indeed anyone, he wanted. I have no doubt that his plan was hatched even before inviting us to work for him. We'd had a lucky escape thanks to the honesty of Mr Walters to whom I am eternally grateful. It was a delight to see Alkema slink away defeated. We continued to get paid and went on to make Holland our home.

Within a couple of months we found premises in Leeuwarden, an old supermarket, laid a maple floor, put in mirrors and a glitter ball and opened our own dance school 'Lloyd's Dance', private lessons all day and classes in the evenings, just like the old days. It was there that I received a phone call from Marion Brown at The Mardi telling me that my beloved teacher, friend and surrogate mother Miss Haylor had died suddenly from a heart attack.

The only solace I could find was, as with Patric, I had got to say my goodbyes. I sent flowers to Nerina who I knew would be broken hearted. It put my recent troubles in perspective. Not long after we began travelling to Germany and France teaching and judging Ballroom, Latin and the soon to become Freestyle Disco. I was asked to judge the French Ballroom and Latin American Championships and spent three days in Paris teaching. The French Champions Michelle and Odile Offrea took a group of us to lunch. I was enjoying the chicken wings when Michelle started to croak like a frog. I immediately retched. They all found it side splittingly funny.

Back in Holland Alyson formed a team of Disco dancers from our students, trained them and designed their costumes and they too became very much in demand. As if that wasn't enough we formed a Ballroom and Latin American team which we took overseas, including the UK for matches, all the while still running our school. How the hell we did it I don't know but we were young and full of energy and loved what we were doing. My mother, Nan and brothers Paul and Stewart loved coming out to Holland for holidays with us. They disliked the ferry crossing from Harwich to the Hook, which could often be very rough, but it was worth it because when they got to us we spoiled them rotten. After our first year in Holland, Alyson and I were nominated for The Action Sports Peak Award to mark our contribution to dance. We won it!! We had risen from the despair of the court case to the ecstasy of seemingly unstoppable success. It was a magical time. We didn't know it at the time of course but those wonderful years in Holland were also to be our swansong as professional dance teachers.

Chapter 11

'Disco Inferno'

Holland 12th May 1982 our son Craig was born. This very special moment changed our lives and soon the decision was made to return to the UK to be closer to the little fella's grandparents. We arrived home in January 1983 and stayed with my mum in Essex for a short while until we bought a house of our own. Back in Holland one of our pupils Omar Smids started his own dance school keeping our name so the Lloyd legacy lived on but the dance world at home was not welcoming. Phyllis Haylor and Patric Plumb, my dearest friends and mentors, had both sadly passed away and Sydney hadn't forgiven me for going to Holland. I went to London to see Bill Irvine, we had a catch up and I told him about a job that I had decided to apply for, Manager of Thorpe Hall Golf Club, which was near to our new house. Bill was surprised and asked me why I wasn't going to continue with my teaching career. I told him a half truth, that I just felt like a change for a while but I intended to resume teaching at some future date. Bill kindly provided me with the best possible reference on his impressive headed paper. The last line read 'I am very confident that George Lloyd would be very successful in any position for which he applied, and an asset to your business. Bill Irvine MBE.' That's what I call impressive!

I arrived for my interview at Thorpe Hall to be greeted by the club secretary, Major Phillip Conibear. After a brief but pleasant chat I handed over my glowing reference from Bill which he scanned with interest. There was a form to complete and I did so together with the other thirty or so applicants waiting in the bar area. We were called in for interviews one by one. I waited and waited, kicking my heels and getting more and more nervous, and yes, they left me till last. The Major took me in to meet the board of directors. This was my first ever interview outside the dance world and to be honest I knew nothing about managing a golf club. I just made up answers to their questions on the spot, the first thing that came into my head in fact. I told them there had been a licensed bar in our dance school in Holland and at The Mardi but withheld the tale of my being barred for underage drinking. I didn't think it would help. I honestly can't remember any of my other replies but they seemed clumsy and unconvincing to me. The directors were headed by a high court judge, Frank Lockhart and millionaire entrepreneur Frank Gammon. The porcine link gave me hope. The grilling came to an end and I was asked to wait back in the bar. Five minutes later all five directors joined me there and the Major announced that my application had been successful. I was now the new house manager of Thorpe Hall Golf Club. You could have knocked me down with feather. Drinks began to flow. The conversation was pleasant and relaxed. It was very like the social atmosphere when judging dance only one of today's judges was of the Wig and Robes variety. The soiree went on until late as Frank Gammon, now under the influence, revealed that he loved ballroom dancing and he and his wife had had lessons with Peter Varley in Leigh on Sea. They had taken the bronze, silver and gold medal tests so they were obviously serious about it. He told me that he had attended a gala ball at Runnymede Leisure Centre in 1974 where he saw me give a Latin American exhibition on the same evening as Bill and Bobbie Irvine did the ballroom show. By now it was becoming clearer and clearer how I'd got the job. Just like the pros on Strictly Come Dancing demonstrating your abilities can open up doors that would otherwise remain closed.

At around midnight with only three of us left standing Frank, now unable to drive his new gold Rolls Royce the five hundred yards to his own front door, handed me the keys and asked me to put it in his drive for him then staggered off across the ninth green into his own back garden. I found it odd that he would bother to use his car when his house was just spitting distance away. The Major explained that Frank always arrived in his Rolls Royce, it was a status symbol, and one of my regular jobs would be to make sure it got home safely as Frank 'liked a drink or two.' Driving Frank's car brought back memories of the showroom in Park Lane where I stood as a boy looking at all the Rollers and Bentleys dreaming that one day I might drive or even own, one!!! The Major said I could play golf free of charge whenever the mood took me. I told him that I had never so much as seen a game of golf let alone played one and he offered to teach me which he did. He was a very kind man and we were to become good friends. I said goodnight and shot off back home. I couldn't wait to tell Alyson and my mum the news. They had already guessed and assumed correctly that I had been held up at the nineteenth hole. We had a nightcap to celebrate. It had been a memorable day.

About a week later at around eight AM there was a loud knock on my front door accompanied by a voice shouting 'Open up. We've got a warrant!' I obeyed the instruction and found two police officers and two customs officials on my doorstep. They showed me their badges and a warrant entitling them to seize my car. I handed them the keys all the time protesting that it must be a mistake of some kind. My pleas were ignored and they declined to give me any more information other than that my car would be impounded at the HMRC compound in Southend on Sea. When I arrived at the golf club later that morning I told the Major what had happened and he immediately got on the blower to Frank the QC and related the story. Within the hour my car was returned to me at the golf club with an apology. Frank came to the club that evening and explained that they had taken the vehicle by mistake. Apparently the police had been watching a certain garage they suspected of being involved in drug smuggling. The garage was on the corner of the road where my mum lived, and the previous day I'd taken my car there with an electric window fault. They stripped the inside door panel and fixed it while I waited. The police watching the place saw me turn up in a left hand drive Chevrolet Caprice classic with Dutch number plates and believed that the criminals, of whom I was an accomplice, had put a consignment of drugs in the door panel ready for me to drive it back to Amsterdam and acted accordingly. 'George Lloyd, international drug smuggler!' It had a ring to it but they'd got the wrong man. They had already checked the panel by the time Frank rang and then thanks to his exalted position the matter was expedited post haste. It is good to have friends in high places.

My job at the club included planning special events such as gala dinner dances with entertainment, weddings and private parties. It was relatively straightforward until one day the chef called in sick. We had a function booked for four hundred people, twenty waitresses but no chef. Well I had grown to enjoy cooking at home for the family and seeing there was no obvious alternative I bit the culinary bullet, put on some whites, and headed for the kitchen. It was big enough to hold dance classes in. There was no time for self indulgent pondering so, with the expert help of the kitchen staff, I got on with it. It was like being back in The Albert Hall, no idea how I got there but too late to back out and you know somehow by the grace of god we got it done, the entire four courses as described on the menu and there was not a single word of complaint from any of the diners including the Lord Mayor and guest of Honour the actor Reg Varney. There were even some compliments to the chef! Following the meal Reg, famous from the hugely successful sitcom 'On the Bus's', played the piano to entertain the gathering. He was incredibly good, a talent no-one knew he possessed. It was a memorable evening, one of many at this prestigious golf club and after that baptism of fire I got involved in the kitchen quite regularly.

Following my time at the golf club we opened a new restaurant in Thorpe Bay named 'On Broadway'. It had tables placed around the perimeter leaving the entire floor available for cabaret and dancing. We employed a very young and talented Spanish singer guitarist called Juan Acevedo who serenaded the customers several nights a week with his love songs in the style of Julio Iglesias. We also held Spanish nights once a month with paella and a female Flamenco dancer. On the first of such nights the show began and what with the music, the dance and the wine I couldn't resist. Yes, you guessed it, the Chef, yours truly, made an unscheduled appearance during the show. The audience and the dancer were amazed. We performed an unrehearsed Flamenco duet, very spontaneous and great fun. It brought the house down. The story made the local newspapers and our Spanish nights were fully booked in advance. My castanets were always at the ready!

In 1985 we sold our house and refurbished The Queens Head pub in Southminster. This included creating a large outdoor barbecue area to the rear of the building which attracted hundreds of customers on summer weekends. The place became extremely popular. My old friend Neil Oliver, a very successful ballroom dancer who had started out with me at The Western, worked for us as bar manager. It was hectic but work wise, compared to dance teaching, it was a walk in the park and Alyson, Craig and I had lovely living quarters. We also had a lovely little dog called Lucky but he wanted for a companion so I got dispatched to Battersea Dogs Home to find him one. I found Queenie another small cross breed. She looked as though she'd be a perfect girlfriend. Lucky could soon be living up to his name. Then just as I was leaving I spotted a bony, half starved, very sad looking, grey Great Dane in a cage on his own. The staff told me that it was his last day. He had been beaten and neglected and nobody wanted him because he was so big. They were putting him down tomorrow. Well I couldn't have that, no way, not after the way he looked at me with those beautiful, mournful eyes. We had an empty caravan to the side of the pub which would be a perfect kennel for a big lad like him. I returned home with two new additions to the family rather than the one I had set out for and Alyson and Craig were delighted. Lucky, Queenie and Duke were very happy together as we were with them. Listen, about Duke, how anyone, no matter how stupid or brutish, could treat an innocent, sweet, trusting creature as he had been treated defies my understanding. They disgust me more than I can express in words. Damn them.

Due to our culinary success at the Queens Head the owners, Grand Metropolitan, asked if I would represent them in the Paglesham Oyster Festival, I kid you not there is such a thing, where I would be required to compete against other chefs to create a new seafood dish. I agreed then forgot about it until a few months later when the director called me to say that he would be attending the festival the next day, looked forward to seeing me and good luck. There was to be no food preparation in advance as everything had to be done in the kitchen at the venue in front of the judges. Panic stations! I got up early the next morning and high-tailed it down to Dengie Shellfish in Burnham on Crouch where I bought fresh mussels, prawns, langoustines and cod, two large fish platters from the gift shop and one of everything from the greengrocers. From there I dashed back to the pub to grab a bottle or three of wine and my freshly ironed chef's jacket and then, after a kiss from my beloved and with no idea whatsoever what I was going to concoct, I shot off to the Oyster Festival. Uncle Jim and Auntie Rina turned up at the venue, a large pub in Paglesham, to cheer me on. The competing chefs had shared use of the kitchen so conditions were not ideal but tallyho! The seafood dish I eventually put together included the entire contents of a bottle of red wine. The cod took on the appearance of beetroot. In fact all the seafood turned a brilliant red and, served on a bed of a by then pink white rice, the entire meal looked like the chef had cut himself and bled profusely into it. There was no time to change anything though so I pressed ahead and served it on a glass platter with buckets full of parsley and wedges of lemon next to a second platter containing every salad item known to man. My work being done I stood back and enjoyed a glass of dry white from one of the other bottles I'd brought with me, the one that my langoustines should have been swimming in, waste not want not. I'm sure that Rick Stein would have been horrified at my 'Lloyd on Fish recipe'. Oh shit here come the judges! They were accompanied by a well known food writer and critic and a BBC Radio live broadcast team who were interviewing each contestant and tasting the delights on offer one by one. Next to mine was a spectacular looking salmon mousse which looked amazing. Then they got to me. With a microphone thrust directly under my nose I was asked the name of my dish. By now somewhat under the influence and never having given a thought to the question I said the first thing that came into my head, 'Mussels Valencia'! They tasted it and asked about the ingredients. This was a bit more complicated but I stumbled through them with relative lucidity claiming that the surfeit of red vino was intentional. When the results were decided the winner of that year's Paglesham Oyster Festival was George Lloyd. I was stunned and incoherent as they handed me a cheque and a large silver cup. I was even more stunned however when the food critic asked me if he could put the recipe for Mussels Valencia in his new book!

In 1985 my mother developed a worrying cough and was diagnosed with lung cancer. Alyson looked after the business and took care of Stewart while I drove my mum to have major surgery at the London Chest Hospital where they removed most of the left lung. I stayed with her day and night for several weeks. Thank god she made a good recovery and life returned to normal. The cough returned two years later however and we returned to the hospital for further tests.

My Nan and Granddad were there too as the seriousness of the situation was apparent. Mum went in to get the results of the tests on her own. I'd offered to go in with her but she declined. She came out with a look on her face I will never forget. As we made our way from the building I asked her what the doctor had said but she didn't want to discuss it at the time. In fact she never discussed it. The only thing she ever did was to ask Alyson to promise that we would look after Stewart for her. Of course she did. In fact Mum and Stewart moved in immediately so we could take care of them both. It soon became clear that mum need specialist care however and we managed to find a wonderful place called Fairhaven in Westcliffe on Sea for her. Her room had French windows that opened out onto a lovely flower garden. We'd sit there together talking about the past, the family and my childhood. It was a most precious time. Mum passed away in Fairhaven in the early hours of a warm summer morning in 1988. Nan and I were by her side. We cried together until there were no tears left. I reverted back to a state of depression just as I had when dad died. My family did all they could to console and comfort me but I was in a bad place. Alyson became very concerned and at one point even thought I was on the brink of ending it all. Everyone has their own way of dealing with life's traumas. In some cases I can be very strong but on this occasion my emotions took over and I crumbled. Mum was buried with my Dad so they were finally reunited. In time with the help and love of my family my life got back on track. I owe so much to them. Shortly after mum's funeral we made the decision to move to Wales to be nearer Alyson's Mum and Dad.

We bought a house in Swansea and on 25th January 1990 our daughter Jamie Molly was born. She was the prettiest baby that ever was. Our family was complete. We invested in several gastro pub restaurants and things were going well, then tragedy struck. I fell down a flight of stairs and landed with tremendous force on my right foot. My knee shattered into pieces. Surgeons tried to piece it back together using metal plates and screws but the outcome wasn't good. After the operation a blood clot went to my lung and nearly killed me. Following a long stay in hospital I was taken home on a stretcher. Now bedridden and told by the surgeons that I would never again be able to bend my right leg, which was also now two centimetres shorter than my left, I realised that my dancing career was well and truly over. Shortly after his sixteenth birthday my brother Stewart decided that he wanted to track down his father and left our home in Wales to stay with my Auntie Rina and Uncle Jim in Essex. I couldn't argue with his wishes, after all I had left home at sixteen. He had our blessing. A few years later he got married to a nurse and we all attended the wedding. I arranged the wedding cars as part of our gift to the happy couple. It was a lovely day with all the extended family in attendance but I was secretly pleased to note no Mister Wonderful. Once a creep always a creep I reckoned.

Prior to this, just after Stewart left in fact, while I was still in bed with my shattered knee, a fire broke out downstairs in the middle of the night. Alyson got the kids out of bed and led them out with the dogs but I was trapped in our bedroom unable to stand up, the flames spread so fast Alyson could do nothing. I was choking on the black smoke, I was sure that this was it. They say your life flashes before you and they are right. It was like a pictorial review of the greatest highlights, my childhood, mum and dad, dancing in the pig farm, London, dance schools, my darling Alyson and my lovely children then, in the midst of this strange state, between life and death, I was suddenly overwhelmed by sense of profound calm. I had heard of this happening to people who were drowning or freezing in an Arctic wasteland and now it was happening to me. Like them I'd accepted what was to come and surrendered to it. I was a child in my mother's arms again. Then for some reason I opened my eyes and looked up to see two fire-fighters stood there in the impenetrable smoke next to my bed. They put an oxygen mask over my face then lifted me up and carried me down the burning hallway to the rear of the property. The fire had engulfed the main staircase so there was no way to the ground floor. I was then carried down extending ladders to an ambulance that was waiting outside with the Fire engines and police. Alyson and the children were overwhelmed with relief that I'd got out, even the dogs were happy to see me, jumping up and barking with delight. The courage of these brave men brings tears to my eyes in remembering it even now. What a wonderful thing to do, to appear in the hellish smoke like angels and save a human life like that. I will be forever grateful.

After a short check up at the hospital, where they found me without serious effects from the incident, we booked into The Dolphin Hotel, where we had stayed on our wedding night 13 years earlier. Lucky, Queenie and Duke had been taken in by neighbours. I slept like a baby. The next morning Alyson borrowed a track suit and trainers and went to buy us some emergency clothing, footwear and toothbrushes from town. We stayed in temporary accommodation for less than a month then moved into a house in nearby Gowerton. It took some time but we gradually got over the nightmare of the fire and the loss of many treasured personal possessions. You can imagine the enormity of the trauma but thank god we were all unharmed. I carried on working hard with my physiotherapist but I was finding it difficult to come to terms with my leg injury. I'd accepted I wouldn't be able to dance again but the thought that I would never even be able to walk properly again was devastating. That said I was determined to prove them wrong. They said I would never bend the leg again but I had already achieved 50%, still a long way to go but I wouldn't let it defeat me. The accident, the fire, it was as if someone had it in for me. When sorrows come they tend to come in threes. The next one made the first two pale into insignificance. Our five year old daughter Jamie Molly became ill and was diagnosed with Cancer, Acute Lymphoblastic Leukaemia. It happened so fast, one minute we were just a normal happy family then total devastation. It affected all of us in equal measures. We were rushed to Llandough hospital in Cardiff. I carried Jamie in from the ambulance as she was too weak to walk. When we entered the ward it was like stepping into a Dickensian nightmare. There were rows of dimly lit beds, one on either side, holding tiny children with no hair and dark sunken eyes, some with thin tubes taped to their pale little faces, all frail and pleading wordlessly for help. I felt that we were walking our little girl into the valley of the shadow of death. I wanted to scream and turn and run but this was our only chance. I felt physically sick but I had to control it, to hide it. I had to be strong. Jamie was so unwell that she was unaware of what was happening. Treatment started immediately. During the first week she started to lose her hair then she sat up in bed one morning and said "Daddy please cut off my hair." I carried her to a side room put her long beautiful hair in a ballet snood and cut it off. I cried inwardly and swallowed my tears. Within another week or so she was completely bald. After we had been in the hospital for six weeks we were allowed to take her home for a time. Jamie didn't want to wear a wig and when she was well enough she couldn't wait to go back to school. That first morning she decided to remove her hat in the assembly and show all the children that she had no hair. They were very accepting and supportive of her. It was touching to see. After two years of chemotherapy Jamie was in remission and looking forward to her life getting back to normal. Her hair was growing back nicely. She was just seven years old. We were home as a family again. Our son Craig had been at the hospital with us most of the time, going to stay with his grandparents every now and then for a break but now, at last, we were all together again looking forward to the future. Seeing your child being struck down with a monstrous, often fatal, disease like that is the worst thing that can happen to a person, nothing compares. The helplessness of watching them suffer, seeing their fear and confusion, their tears, their little acts of bravery knowing there's nothing you can do about it. It cuts you deep. Why her? Why not me? I cannot tell you of the mental and spiritual anguish we as a family went through. I cursed the god I prayed to. It had passed though. She had recovered. Surely this would be an end to our run of tragedies. Then a routine blood test showed the cancer had returned with a vengeance and our whole world just fell apart again.

Chapter 12

'Candle in the Wind'

Jamie would need to undergo two more years of chemotherapy plus cranial radiotherapy. The despair that I had already experienced came back magnified. I was stepping back into the nightmare. Later that day we had a meeting with the consultant David Webb and he gave us the prognosis. Odds on survival had dropped from the initial 85% to 25%. He said that if the chemotherapy didn't work we would then be looking at a bone marrow transplant. A donor would have to be found and the first port of call would be within the family. Alyson found this particularly stressful as she was adopted and had had no contact with her birth family, one of who could be the perfect match. We applied for access to her adoption papers where we found her birth parents names. I decided to try to trace the whereabouts of her mother without Alyson knowing. If I found her and she didn't want to know I could tell Alyson I couldn't trace her thus saving her the further trauma of rejection. Alyson was born in Swansea and had been adopted from Cwmdonkin House Orphan's Home in the city. It only took me a few hours to trace her. Alyson's mother's name was Mera Scott and her father's Patrick Sweeney. I searched the birth records and found Mera Scott then searching further I discovered her marriage certificate to Patrick Sweeney in Darlington.

I looked through the BT phone records and found their number. I thought about how to approach this potentially explosive situation and decided to at first pretend I was a double glazing salesman making a random call. This shows how crazy I was. I made the call, introduced myself as a rep calling from South Wales and asked if I could speak to Mera Scott. The lady who'd picked up the phone said it was her but her married name was Sweeney. Then to my utter amazement she said that she knew why I was calling. She said it was about her daughter Collette who she'd had adopted. I confirmed this and said she was now called Alyson and she was my wife. It was an extremely emotional conversation. I told her about Jamie and why I had had to find her. She said that she had married Alyson's father and Alyson now had four other full blood siblings. I have to admit that despite the drama my only real concern at this point was finding potential bone marrow donors for Jamie and to protect Alyson so this news was wonderful, that said Mera was very sweet and I could feel her warmth and caring nature even over the telephone. When we eventually met my initial thoughts were confirmed. She was a very special, loving, selfless woman who we grew to love. We also met the rest of Alyson's newly discovered family, her father Patrick, brothers Andrew and John and sisters Patricia and Susan plus all the nephews and nieces. It was a beautiful reunion. Thank god we never had to ask for donors but knowing they were there, ready and willing, was very reassuring.

For the time being though we had to battle on and try to focus on the positive. It was very difficult. We were back to the old routine of long stays in hospital, Alyson sleeping every night on a camp bed next to Jamie and Craig and me in hospital accommodation provided by the Welsh children's cancer charity 'LATCH' which was started there at Llandough where Jamie was being treated.

In the Christmas of 1995, less than a year after Alyson's brother Michael was diagnosed with cancer of the mouth he underwent major surgery to remove his tongue which was replaced with a flap taken from his forearm. It was a horrible experience for him but at least he was still with us for a short while longer. He died in February of 1996. He was forty-six years old. Alyson was distraught at his death, they had grown up together and she felt as if she'd lost a part of herself. She showed great courage and fortitude however caring for her parents and supporting Jamie through her chemotherapy despite her personal pain.

Comedian and actor Stan Stennett MBE and patron of LATCH became a close friend. Alyson and I became involved and organised many charity events in aid of LATCH and we were delighted and grateful to receive the support of a bevy of famous people, Sir Tom Jones, Rhys Ifans, Shakin' Stevens, Bonnie Tyler, Larry King, Doris Day, Paul Whitehouse, Dame Shirley Bassey, Boyd Clack, Brian Hibbard, Joe Calzaghe, Kevin Allen, Charlotte Church, Lily Allen, John Travolta, Richard and Judy Madeley, Shane Richie, Phil Collins, and many more. Whilst many artists were generous, there were two men that went that step further, my dear friends Flying Pickets Singer, Actor Brian Hibbard and Actor, Writer, Singer-Song writer Boyd Clack, both giving freely of their time at charity events, singing on the karaoke, playing pool with the kids, and making everyone laugh. Very sadly Brian passed away in 2012. Since then Boyd has continued to support LATCH by attending events together with his lovely partner, Writer and Actor Kirsten Jones. Boyd and Kirsten have become very close friends. In fact Boyd and I are like brothers we have a very deep connection and are very similar in many ways. Simple to explain really "I just love the man".

It became clear to me that LATCH would benefit by raising its profile.

When I talked it through with Alyson she came up with the idea of contacting Princess Diana who was already known for her devoted work for many other charities. I thought it was an inspired idea so Alyson sat down and wrote a letter straight from her heart telling the Princess all about Jamie and what we were going through as a family. She didn't ask for anything for us or Jamie, she simply asked Diana to support LATCH. To my amazement we received a telephone call from Kensington Palace the very next day; the ink had barely had time to dry. They confirmed that Princess Diana was not only happy to support LATCH but she would be very happy to visit the charity in Cardiff and would like to bring Prince William and Prince Harry with her. I was lost for words. I started to stutter out a response when suddenly there were screams of laughter at the other end of the phone. I stood there and listened – I could hear a man in the back ground talking fast and still all the laughter. I didn't know what was going on. Eventually I said "Hello I'm still here" at which the lady on the other end of the phone composed herself and said "I'm so sorry Mr Lloyd but Michael Barrymore has just arrived and he's making the Princess laugh." It was the most surreal phone call I'd ever had. Anyway over the next few days arrangements for the visit were put into place. I met with the Lord Lieutenant and the Special Police security in Cardiff and everything was planned to the finest detail. The Princess would arrive on 2nd Sept 1997 at Cardiff Docks 10.45 am by helicopter and then be driven to Llandough Hospital in an armoured convoy. Jamie was to present a posy to the Princess at 11am and later on departure two Welsh Dragons for Prince William and Prince Harry. As if this wasn't exciting enough we then received a personal invitation from

Princess Diana for the family to go and have a private tea with her at Kensington Palace. She was keen for her boys to meet Jamie and our son Craig who was the same age as William. The date was fixed for Wednesday 3rd September 1997. On Friday 29th August 1997 a bouquet of beautiful pink flowers, roses, carnations and lilies arrived at our house for Jamie. The hand written card read "To dearest Jamie, Its lovely to know you're now at home and I hope that you and your family will be able to come and see me very soon but until then lots of love from Diana". Just two days later the Princess was dead.

When the news broke in the early hours the media went crazy, unbeknown to us Robin Wayne, the florist that delivered the bouquet had contacted Swansea Sound, the local radio station, in response to them asking over air if anyone had any interesting memories of the Princess, and told them about the delivery of the bouquet which was deemed to be Diana's last act of kindness. The next day, the Monday, Swansea Sound and Evening Post contacted us for interviews and the next morning we were on the radio and there was a front page article in the Post. That morning we did a telephone interview with BBC Radio Five Live and later in the day a Daily Mail journalist turned up with a photographer. The article with a lovely photo of Jamie on page two of Wednesday's Mail produced a flood of phone calls from Radio and TV stations from all over the country and abroad, ITN, BBC, Channel 4, S4C, HTV, Sky News, CNN, Good Morning America, ABC News, Richard and Judy, Radio Dublin and many more, asking for interviews. A number of their outside broadcasting wagons congregated outside our house. The first to knock on the door was ITV's Tim Rogers. While waiting for the crew to set up, Alyson hit upon an idea, how about getting them to pay for the interviews. They were TV companies and therefore loaded after all and all the money would go to LATCH. It was another example of how much more intelligent and astute my wife is than me. I gave her a kiss and opened the door. We conducted the interviews in our front room. Alyson made sure all their payments went straight into the LATCH bank account. News at Ten, Channel Four News, S4C, Sky News, Channel Five. We screwed them all in a good cause.

Then things moved on one step further, Richard and Judy, Good Morning Britain, Good Morning America, and Larry King Live had all invited us to appear on their respective shows, so after agreeing that we could talk about LATCH in the interviews and there would be donations made, we made our way to London and arrived at The Westbury Hotel in Mayfair just after midnight. Just an hour later a limo arrived to take us to a TV studio where at 3AM we had a live interview via satellite with Larry King Live on CNN. This was broadcast there and then around the world to two hundred and sixty countries, three thousand six hundred major cities and six hundred million people. I must have name dropped LATCH Cardiff a hundred times. Every time they asked a question I included the word LATCH in the reply, for example Larry King asked "George you were going to have tea with the Princess weren't you?" "Yes that's right Larry the day after she was going to visit the Welsh Children's Cancer Charity LATCH in Cardiff she did invite us to tea". It may have been a bit obvious and clumsy but I didn't care. Whilst Jamie and I were live on air the donations were pouring in. In the green room before the interview Larry's team had been chatting to Jamie about her favourite things and she had told them she loved the film 'Grease' and the dreamboat John Travolta was her idol. Unbeknown to us CNN were trying to contact John Travolta so they could arrange a satellite link with him to surprise Jamie during the interview. Unfortunately he was flying his Jet at that very time. Ah well. We didn't mention it to her to save her from the inevitable disappointment. We returned to the hotel by 4 AM and got some much needed shut eye. I was woken at around 8.30 AM by the phone ringing. The desk receptionist said we had a long distance call from Mr John Travolta and she was putting us through. I managed to croak out a strangled hello and he said "Good morning I'm sorry that I was unable to link up with you and Jamie earlier but my head was in the clouds so I'm calling now to talk to her if that's okay". There was so much I wanted to say but I looked at Jamie's little face and realised this was her moment so I just said "Of course." and handed her the phone. They talked for around twenty minutes about all kinds of things. Her face was a picture, he promised to send her a present which he did, a box containing his own personal signed copy of a 'Grease' VHS with CBS seal intact, a selection of private signed photos that have never been published and a private tape recording of a children's story written and voiced by him for his own son together with a personal hand written letter explaining all of the above. This lovely gesture and the time he gave Jamie meant such a lot to her, and I am convinced it had a very positive mental affect on her battle with cancer. It was a beautiful and generous thing he did. It amazes people that given the chance to talk to John I didn't explain the effect he had had on my life, that after seeing him in Saturday Night Fever I was responsible for spreading the word throughout not only Britain but most of Europe as well. Well it amazes me too but the situation wasn't right for me to go into it at that time. If he ever rings again I assure you I will bore the incredibly tight black velvet pants off him.

The rest of the day was taken up with further interviews at various locations all over the city including another live one with Good Morning America outside Buckingham Palace. Before returning to the hotel we called in at a florist in Brewer Street to collect flowers for a LATCH tribute bouquet. After that we had a lovely dinner and an early night. We needed it.

Friday 5th up at crack of dawn for breakfast then picked up and taken to the Richard and Judy Good Morning Show. After makeup we had coffee in the green room in the company of Sir Trevor McDonald who was charm itself. The interview was at midday then the three of us signed the official book of condolences on behalf of LATCH and were driven back to Buckingham Palace to place the flowers from the charity at the gates along with the mountain of other floral tributes already there. Jamie also placed four pink roses from the bouquet Diana had sent her among them. The card, which she wrote herself, read "To Dear Princess Diana, although I never got to have tea with you I know you are looking down. You were an angel before but now you've got wings. There are four of your favourite roses from the bouquet you sent me, one for you, one for Dodi, one for Prince William and one for Prince Harry. I love you and miss you. xxxxxxxx"

We drove back home to Swansea and had another early night. On the Saturday we had a phone call from Dr Eileen Thompson MBE, Consultant paediatric oncologist, the founder of LATCH to thank us for representing them and say that they had been receiving donations from all over the world. There was even a team lead by a woman named Shirley raising money for us in Washington DC. Good had come out of this tragedy, something I think Diana would have been very happy about. Sadly I never got the chance to ask Princess Diana what she thought of the disco routines of ours that she had learnt all those years ago, or how her dance with John Travolta compared to mine but more importantly the chance to thank her for the kindness that she showed towards our little girl Jamie who has survived against all the odds. 'Thank you our Queen of Hearts. X'

The death of Diana sent the whole nation into shock and made people stop and think about what really matters in life. Jamie's recovery and the welfare of sick children really mattered and our charity work continued with extra drive. As well as for LATCH Alyson decided to raise funds and awareness for the Welsh Children's Hospice Ty Hafan in Cardiff. Around that time I contacted a large number of garages in South Wales asking for a new car for Lee Evans from Port Talbot, a seventeen year old boy who'd been having cancer treatment for several years. After many negative responses Gills of Maesteg came up trumps and provided the lad with a spanking new Ford Fiesta. Stan Stennett joined us for the presentation and Lee's delight was a joy to behold. Unfortunately this lovely, sweet boy passed away in his twenties. Dr. Thompson asked me to join the executive committee of LATCH which I was honoured to do. Incidentally Dr. Thompson could have been my ballroom mentor Miss Haylor's twin sister. They were both elegant, successful ladies with a tendency to mother me and keep me in line. I was still the joker and needed the occasional tug on my leash.

In 2000, the year of the Millennium, Alyson's father Philip suddenly became unwell. Wyn nursed him at home but it gradually took its toll and she found herself urgently in need of respite so we arranged a place in a nursing home for Phil while Wyn moved in with us. The dear man passed away peacefully in his sleep within a couple of weeks and sadly, as is often the case with couples who had been married for a long time, Wyn died a month later. They were buried together. Alyson and I had no doubt that the tragically early death of their son Michael and their subsequent broken hearts had contributed a great deal to their mutual decline. Their deaths made Alyson relate closely to my despair after my parents died. Her parents were much older when they adopted her and, as I did with my father, she too felt cheated by time and fate. Her love for her family was total and uncomplicated. We mourned their loss together.

As the years passed Jamie's health went from strength to strength. Now fourteen years old and in remission for five years, life was getting back to normal. Alyson and I were more relaxed and confident that the worst was now behind us. The next event came as a bolt from the deepest blue. I found Alyson sitting on the bed staring at a plastic thermometer and I immediately panicked my heart missing a beat thinking that Jamie had spiked a temperature. Alyson was pregnant! It was a pregnancy tester not a thermometer! It wasn't planned and we were a bit concerned about our ages, she was forty-four and I was forty-nine, but, though shocked at first, we accepted this gift in good heart. I couldn't help but feel excited and it wasn't long before Alyson felt the same. We talked it through, embraced it and began to plan our newly sketched out future with this unexpected but very welcome addition to our family in the starring role. The weeks passed quickly and we went for the first scan. Seeing the little one, the tiny life we had created, was emotional for both of us. It was magical, the only real magic. We were very happy. We felt blessed. Jamie was looking forward to having a new brother or sister too. Over the next weeks we planned the nursery and discussed names. Time was speeding up. The date for the twenty week scan arrived, hopefully we could find out whether it was a boy or a girl this time. We watched on as the nurse studied the screen and asked her if she could tell the sex. She paused without replying, excused herself for a moment and left the room. A few minutes later she returned with the consultant who continued with the procedure. I was concerned by this time and asked him if there was a problem. He replied that there was no heart beat. The baby was dead. Alyson's eyes filled with tears. Mine ran down my face like acid rain. It was devastating news and now we had to face the unimaginable trauma of having the dear little one delivered. Alyson was given preparatory medication and we were left alone together in a private room. I felt helpless, unable to affect the situation I could only offer my love and support both of which seemed hopelessly inadequate. After the delivery our baby was handed to us in a Moses basket, a beautiful little boy. We named him Harri. He had lovely long legs which would have been perfect for dancing. This was a different kind of grief, the not knowing what could have been, the deep feeling of loss doubled, first coping with the pain of the death of a loved one and secondly the irrational but overwhelming feeling that you had somehow failed the helpless, innocent unborn child. It stays with you forever.

Jamie decided to study to become a nurse and after graduating from university her ambition was realised. She is now a Staff Nurse in Swansea and Alyson and I are grandparents to a baby boy born in 2016. We also have other lovely grandchildren to love and brighten our lives courtesy of our son.

After our time in the restaurant and pub business I decided to try my luck in the motor car trade. In 2002 I started importing and exporting cars and my company GLC Autos was born. With the invaluable help of my son Craig it turned out to be a very lucrative venture. Craig later moved into property development and became a highly successful businessman. Alyson meanwhile teamed up with her old friend Lissa Williams nee James and started teaching dance again. They tried everything to get me involved but my old bones and dodgy knee forced me to politely decline. They flourished nonetheless. It was wonderful to see my beloved so happy doing what she loved again. One day in 2012 a very well dressed gentleman came into the garage and purchased a car. He had a London accent like my own and regaled me with tales of his beloved Fulham football club. I was almost a fan myself by the time he finished. His name was Edward Allen. A few weeks later he returned because he'd found the car not really suitable so he selected another and asked how much he was out of pocket. They were roughly similar prices so I told him to put his cheque book away. It was fine. He was I think pleasantly surprised and since he lived nearby he started calling in the garage regularly for a cuppa and a chat. A few months later I attended the funeral of my friend Brian Hibbard. The service was packed with many of his friends from show business in attendance. Brian was a good and well loved man. A mutual good mate Boyd Clack gave the eulogy which was to say the least, unorthodox. It was the first time I'd ever heard the word 'dogging', which Boyd said Brian had claimed to have invented, at a funeral service. I asked Boyd who the bloke with the suntan and the flash suit was. He said he was a film director he had worked with – Kevin Allen director of the highly success-ful and brilliant film Twin Town (Boyd played the Vicar) and the TV series Benidorm, which explained the suntan. I thought no more of it. Next day my favourite customer and now good friend Edward Allen arrived for a tea and chat in the company of the Miami Vice Hollywood guy from the funeral who was running around the forecourt hysterically demanding the keys to our fastest and most furious cars. Edward informed me that Kevin aka 'Suntan Willie' was his son, brother of actor Keith Allen and uncle of pop star Lily and Game of Thrones actor Alfie. Edward it appeared was patriarch to a dynasty. Ten test drives later Mr Twin Town makes his choice, uneconomical, flash and fast, just what I'd expected. To add to the fiasco I had to take his part exchange, a beaten up, muddy old van he had used and abused on his rare breed pig farm in Ireland. Yes you heard right, Pig Farm. So we had one thing in common at least.

From that day forward Kevin and I became the best of friends and he asked Alyson and me to do the choreography for several films that he was directing and producing. We thoroughly enjoyed the work. It's more or less the same as on 'Strictly Come Dancing', teaching celebrities to dance and many of them have become good friends. Hollywood star Rhys Ifans described his efforts at learning the Rumba for the film Under Milk Wood as like a baby giraffe on ice and on hearing this Boyd Clack, attempting to learn the Tango for the same film, likened himself to Marlon Brando on Spice. I think he was referring to the latter day grossly overweight Brando not the young sex god though with Boyd you can never be sure. Indeed neither Rhys nor Boyd were what you'd call 'naturals' but 'If you can walk, you can dance' being my motto we pressed on and the results weren't at all bad. Working on dance choreography with Alyson again was pure joy and we are booked to do another film for Kevin. I will also be making my acting debut which should be fun.

Kevin seemed to think that my life had been very eventful to say the least – 'colourful' I think he called it, and he encouraged me to put it down in writing, so you can blame him. You just read it!

I have led a charmed life. The dark times have been easily outweighed by the good. I have a family that I love and that loves me. I have had reasonably good health, those I love have surmounted any problems they faced and are now healthy and happy and I have accomplished most of the things I set out to accomplish. You can't ask for any more. My time in the world of dance was a fascinating, often thrilling, occasionally distressing chapter but far from the last. I am still here, alive and not without further ambitions and desires and I wouldn't mind betting that the very best is yet to come. George Lloyd.

PS Princess Diana's bouquet of pink flowers, minus the four roses, is in a glass case at the end of our entrance hall in the very same house they were delivered to where we live to this day.

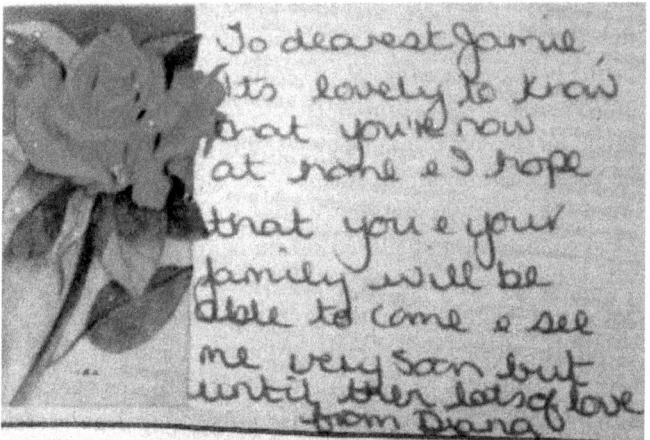

Star phone call for thrilled Jamie

FILM star John Travolta has rung seven-year-old Gowerton leukaemia sufferer Jamie Molly Lloyd.

The top actor, who danced with Diana, Princess of Wales, made the call yesterday morning after hearing Jamie talk of her grief at the princess's death on an American television show.

Jamie's father, George, said: "She couldn't believe it. The call just blew her away.

"She is walking on air at the moment. We never knew things would snowball the way they have after the Post broke the news that Jamie was to have met the Princess."

The superstar, who shot to fame in the movie Saturday Night Fever, has pledged to send Jamie some personal souvenirs.

"Jamie is a big fan and this was a tremendous gesture. He got our number from American television people. It is really humbling when people go so far out of their way to be so kind," said George, of Porth-y-Waun.

Little Jamie was today in London waiting to lay three pink roses at St James's Palace.

Jamie and Diana were to have met in private next week.

THRILLED: Jamie Lloyd.

CALL: John Travolta.

My Thanks

I would like to thank some very important people who have worked hard behind the scenes whilst I took time out to work on this book.

MIKE AND VALERIE DAVIES who have been close friends since 1990. They have supported us through some very difficult times also playing a big role in our charity raising efforts. Mike is always by my side taking care of day to day personal business. He is my right arm, a true friend and a man I can trust. Valerie is the best raffle ticket seller in the world. It's a very persuasive skill. You just can't say no to her.

BEN DAVIES, a world pool champion with many professional titles to his name. Ben is Mike and Valerie's son, a young man with a kind heart and a caring nature who, like his parents, is always happy to support our charity work. I have watched him grow up from a little boy to a fine man with his own lovely family.

RICHARD SULLY, my sales manager at GLC Auto's since the beginning.
Richard is a gym bunny. He goes there early every morning then comes to the office for breakfast before opening

up for business normally at about nine thirty. He has two fridges, a microwave oven and every kitchen utensil known to man in our kitchen and gorges himself on endless meals and protein shakes throughout the day. He can often be found taking a nap on the soft leather sofa in the sales office. A customer recently left a review on our web site saying that while he was very happy with his purchase, the sales manager knew nothing about cars. Richard is essentially unemployable and it seems I am stuck with him. I see it as an extension of my charity work. He is one of a kind and it is both our fortunes to have found each other.

Author's Supplement

Aged just sixteen I had already qualified as an Associate with the Imperial Society of Teachers of Dancing.

At the age of just seventeen I went on to learn all the Ballroom and Latin Technique to Fellowship Level from some of the best professional dance teachers in the business.

I thought it would be nice to share a very small synopsis of this knowledge with you.

With my passion for Choreography the knowledge of Technique has proven to be an essential foundation.

Hopefully you will enjoy reading my Strictly Viewers' Guide to Judging.

'One of the best lessons in life is a dance lesson'

George Lloyd

My Strictly Viewers' Guide to Judging

Dance judges look for different things in what they want to see. One judge, for instance, might be especially interested in technique, while another wants to be moved by musicality and expression.

While both factors are obviously important and need to be considered, it can result in couples being marked high or low depending on the judging panels preferences. Leaving the couples wondering what a judge saw to give them particularly high or low marks. The use of a toe when a heel is required can just as easily hurt you in a judge's eyes as a meticulous closing of feet can help.

Obviously on a crowded competition floor the judge sees each couple for only a few seconds, anything that draws the attention, either positively or negatively, could very well be the deciding factor on how you are marked.

Most judges will evaluate the performance honestly and to the best of their ability using their knowledge of dance to deliver the correct result.

The correct hold and positioning of the body when in closed dancing position. The line of the arms should be unbroken from elbow to elbow. Also coming together to form a circle, which remain in correct body position relative to each other.

The stretch of the woman's body upwards and outwards and leftwards into the man's right arm to achieve balance and connection with his frame.

Good posture helps control your body and balance. It allows your partner to connect well to your body in the ballroom dances.

Forming two people's body weights into one, so that leading and following appear effortless, and the dancers are totally in synchronization with each other.

Musicality and expression of the dance, choreography, musical phrasings, also the use of light and shade to create a winning performance.

For instance, in foxtrot, the stealing of time from one step to allow another to hover; or a quick speed of turn in an otherwise slow rumba; or the snap of a head to suddenly freeze and then melt into slowness in tango.

If a couple are not dancing in time with the music, the game is over and no amount of proficiency in any other aspect can overcome this.

The couples need to sell their routine to the audience with enthusiasm, exuding their joy of dancing and confidence in their performance making it look effortless, to show strain or uncertainty is negative.

The most energetic couple normally wins the Jive. But the energy must be controlled, not wild.

Powerful movement is an asset in waltz or foxtrot, but only if it is channelled into the correct swing of the body, and not just by taking big steps. The lilt of the music must be matched by the action of the body.

In a waltz for instance, the dancers' body action must clearly show the influence of the one down beat and two up beats. So the release of power into the beginning of a figure must be controlled and sustained during the rise at the end of the figure.

Attractive well executed lines either curved or straight, enhance the shapes of the figures by stretching of the body from head to toe.

The ability to avoid bumping into other couples by the man changing direction and in some cases the routine, where the lady would be required to follow no matter what, is known as Floorcraft. It shows the command of the couple over their choreography and the ability of the man to choose and lead figures different to their usual work when the necessity presents itself.

The ability to continue dancing without pause when boxed in is essential to winning.

Waltz is a smooth dance, travelling around the line of dance. It is characterized primarily by its rise & fall action.

The shoulders move smoothly, parallel with the floor, not up and down.

The head should turn in the direction of the turn, otherwise the man's head is upright and looking over the right shoulder of the lady

The rise and fall is unique to the waltz. If possible, all the steps in the waltz should be long.

On the first step forward, the weight is taken on the heel, then on to the ball of the foot.

A gradual rise to the toes should be started at the end of the first beat, and continued to the second and third beat of each bar of music.

Lower to the normal position at the end of the third beat by lowering to the heel of the foot carrying the weight.

The slow waltz is danced to music written in 3/4 time,

with 3 beats to a bar of music = 28–30 bars per minute 84–90 beats per minute.

Foxtrot is a smooth dance, travelling around the line of dance. The long walking movements involve a subtle rise & fall action. Turning movements are similar to Waltz, but with a more moderate rise and fall, and more length-wise action.

The Foxtrot originally started with slow and quick steps but soon evolved to include twinkles and chasses.

The Foxtrot is danced to music written in 4/4 time with the first and third beats more heavily accented. It is danced in combinations of slow and quick steps, with each slow step taking two beats and each quick step one beat of music.

Therefore, a dance basic figure in slow, slow, quick, quick rhythm takes one and a half bars of music, while a dance figure in slow, quick, quick rhythm takes one bar of music.

Foxtrot is extremely versatile and can be danced to a variety of musical styles. With 4 beats to a bar foxtrot music has a tempo of 29 to 34 bars per minute 112–120 beats per minute.

Tango also referred to as the "Dance of Love", is a passionate and dramatic dance. It's a dialogue between partners, an expressive form of communication through movements

It's somewhat different from other dances, especially traditional ballroom, but next in popularity behind waltz and foxtrot Dissimilar to those two, it has no rise & fall, no swaying. It's known for quick, sharp movements and a cat-like walking action.

Today, there are many styles of tango. Although many different interpretations have appeared, the two main styles are the ballroom style and the Argentine style. The main difference between the two is that the second one has more sharp, staccato movements and the characteristic head snaps which are totally foreign for the dances coming from Argentina.

Tango is a walking dance, meaning that all the steps are based on walking.

The rhythm is slow, slow, quick, quick, slow. The slow steps consume two beats of music and the quick steps one. Tango music is usually written in 4/4 time (but also in 2/4 time) and played at a tempo of 30–33 beats per minute.

Quickstep usually follows a 4/4 time pattern. The basic feel of the Quickstep is slow-quick-quick, slow-quick-quick, with "slow" taking beats one and two, and "quick-quick" taking beats three and four. Most of the "slow" steps are taken on the heel, while most "quick" steps are taken on the balls of the feet.

The tempo of quickstep dance is rather brisk as it was developed to ragtime era jazz music which is fast-paced when compared to other dance music. Historically my Ballroom mentor Phyllis Haylor played an important part in incorporating the Charleston movements into the Quickstep

Quickstep is danced in 4/4 time to 48–52 bars per minute, or 192–208 beats per minute.

Viennese Waltz is perhaps the most difficult dance to learn. Most beginners will approach it like Slow Waltz, but the amount of rotation and speed of music can prove fatal within just a few steps. On the other hand, many higher level dancers will agree that Viennese Waltz is one of the easiest dances.

Trying to rise and fall is fatal in this dance it will happen naturally but to the very minimum, having learnt the slow waltz with rise and full pupils naturally assume there should be the same amount of rise and full, but there isn't. Too much rise and full in this dance will only result in a clumsy hoping action as the feet come together, there is no time forget it, do not try to rotate just drive forward to cover the floor keep up with the music and let it flow. Viennese Waltz should feel like there is no rotation at all. The problem for many is that they don't understand how to get around their partners, so they try harder and harder, resulting in a lot of rotation and making the dance tough and exhausting. But instead of trying to get around your partner, try travelling through your partner.

Although we must admit that there is a very slight Rise and Fall in Viennese Waltz, the dancer should nevertheless think of the dance as being flat. Rise and Fall will come naturally, and trying to put in slight Rise and Fall too often results in way more than is desirable. Keep your Viennese Waltz flat

Viennese waltz is danced at about 180 beats (58–60 bars) per minute.

Rumba the dance of love, rumba dancers usually embody a sassy, smooth, and sensual demeanor. The move set is very particular in the details but the most important feature is keeping a connection with your partner. The toes should be at a slight diagonal to allow us to achieve our favorite hip movement, Cuban motion, just like in Salsa.

Rumba is the slowest of the competitive international latin styles.

Usually danced to music written in 4/4 time, with four beats to each bar. The basic step is a very simple box step. It consists of three basic steps - two quick side steps and a slow forward or backward step.

The rhythm of the steps is slow, quick, quick. A slow step is danced over two counts of music, while a quick step is danced over one count.

Rumba is a spot dance which means the couple does not travel around the dance floor like in many other dances, but rather stays in one location. It is done to music with slow tempo and emphasizes on hip movements.

Rumba is generally regarded as the "dance of romance", but also known as the "Latin waltz" or the "waltz with a wiggle". Due to its slow rhythm and sensual movements, some call it the most intimate and passionate dance there is.

Rumba is danced in 4/4 time to 23–25 bars per minute, or 92–100 beats per minute.

Cha Cha like so many Latin dances, it originates from Cuba. Originally it was known as a slowed-down mambo or "the triple mambo", because of the three quick steps. In time it evolved into a separate dance and although it was originally known as the cha-cha-cha, the name was shortened to the cha-cha.

Steps in all directions should be taken first with the ball of the foot in contact with the floor, and then with the heel lowering when the weight is fully transferred. When weight is released from a foot, the heel should release first, allowing the toe to maintain contact with the floor. Latin Hip movement is achieved through the alternate bending and straightening action of the knees. In the International Latin style, the weighted leg should be straight. The free leg will bend, allowing the hips to naturally settle into the direction of the weighted leg. As a step is taken, a free leg will straighten the instant before it receives weight. It should then remain straight until it is completely free of weight again. Traditionally the count is 234&1 and

Cha Cha is danced in 4/4 time to 28–30 bars per minute, or 112–120 beats per minute.

Samba is a style of dance and music from Brazil. Most steps are danced with a slight downward bouncing or dropping action. This action is created through the bending and straightening of the knees, with bending occurring on the beats of 1 and 2, and the straightening occurring between. However there shouldn't be considerable bobbing. Also, Samba has a specific hip action, different from that in ballroom Latin dances (Rumba and Cha-Cha-Cha).

The ballroom samba is danced to music in 2/4 or 4/4 time. It uses several different rhythmic patterns in its figures, with cross-rhythms being a common feature. There are also many three-step patterns requiring syncopation.

Samba is danced in 2/4 time to 50 bars per minute, or 100 beats per minute.

Paso Doble originates from Spain. It developed on the basis of movements performed by the matadors during the Bull Fights. In Paso Doble the man (matador) is in focus more than in any other dance. The lady is left with playing a role of a cape ("cappa") the red canvas of the toreador or a bull, depending on circumstances. Paso Doble is one of the most dramatic dances you will ever see.

The hips are held very forward in this dance by both the leaders and followers. You may even tilt your upper body back in order to balance out the forward position of the hips. The spine is stretched up all the time to create a very dramatic and strong look Because of the arrhythmic and staccato nature of the dance, it is usually danced as part of a highly choreographed performance

Paso Doble is a dance of posturing and high gestures by the man, and flowing circular steps around him by the woman. Because the dance was developed in France, the steps to this Spanish dance actually have French names, such as 'chassez cape' (to chase the cape). While most of the steps are technically led with the heel, because of the high posturing there is quite a bit of moving on the balls of the feet.

Paso Doble is danced in 2/4 time to 60–62 bars per minute, or 120–124 beats per minute.

Jive the basic look and feel of jive are that it is performed with lots and lots of energy, with the legs portraying a pumping action. Basic jive consists of two triple steps and a rock step. The jive count begins with the rock step, which is counted "1, 2." The two triple steps are counted "3 and 4" and "5 and 6."

Jive is a very happy, boppy, energetic dance, with plenty of knee-lifting, bending, and rocking of the hips. The fastest of the Latin dances, jive incorporates lots of kicks and flicks, even twirling of the woman, and doesn't move around the dance floor like other dances. Although jive dancers may appear to be moving their feet haphazardly in every direction, the feet are actually well controlled under the body with the knees close together.

In International Style ballroom dancing competition, jive is grouped with the Latin dances but it is danced to Western music, in 4/4 time with 42 bars per 176 beats per minute.

American Smooth is America's interpretation of the traditional form of Ballroom dance.

The Standard Ballroom consists of five dances (Waltz, Tango, Viennese Waltz, Foxtrot, and Quickstep), all danced in hold without lifts.

The main difference between the two is the fact that in Ballroom you are required to dance in a closed position at all times, while Smooth dancers are permitted to dance in both open and closed positions as well as solo. Lifts are also allowed in American Smooth. This difference gives Smooth dancers significantly more freedom of expression than traditional Ballroom dancers.

American Smooth can be a mix of Ballroom, Show, and Latin, making it a choreographers dream due to its immense versatility.

There are some stylistic differences as well. For instance, the Standard Ballroom Foxtrot is dramatically different than the Smooth Foxtrot. In Standard, the Foxtrot is slow and tame, while in Smooth the Foxtrot is upbeat and jazzy.

Though the Tango is also danced in both styles, the Smooth Tango differs from the Standard variation due to its influences from Paso Doble, which is found in the Latin style. The fact that Smooth can dance in both open and closed position essentially makes all the dances distinctively different because there is so much more choreography that is allowed, giving life to both performers' dancing and allowing for ever-evolving interpretations of the styles.

'One of the best lessons in life is a dance lesson'

George Lloyd